cook's library

Vegetarian

cook's library

Vegetarian

This is a Parragon Publishing Book
This edition published in 2003

Parragon Publishing
Queen Street House
4 Queen Street
Bath BA1 1HE, UK

ISBN: 0-75259-956-9

Printed in China

NOTE

This book uses imperial and metric measurements. Follow the same
units of measurement throughout; do not mix imperial and metric.
All spoon measurements are level: teaspoons are assumed to be 5 ml,
and tablespoons are assumed to be 15 ml. Unless otherwise stated,
milk is assumed to be whole, eggs and individual vegetables such as
potatoes are medium, and pepper is freshly ground black pepper.

The times given for each recipe are an approximate guide only because the
preparation times may differ according to the techniques used by different
people and the cooking times may vary as a result of the type of oven used.
The preparation times include chilling and marinating times, where appropriate.

Recipes using raw or very lightly cooked eggs should be
avoided by infants, the elderly, pregnant women, convalescents,
and anyone suffering from an illness.

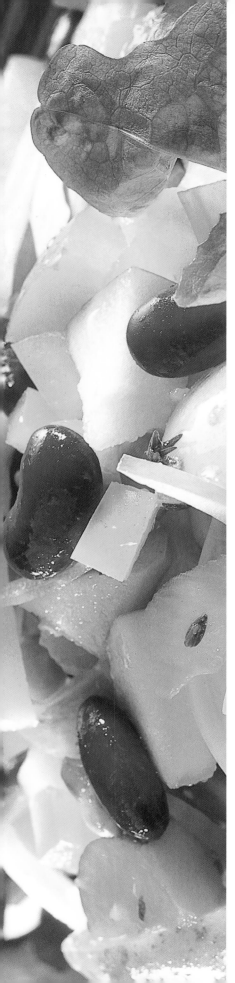

Contents

6   introduction

18   soups

40   appetizers

60   light meals

86   pasta, grains & legumes

112   stir-fries & sautés

128   casseroles & bakes

158   salads

174   index

Introduction

Vegetarian food need not be boring as this inspirational cookbook will demonstrate! Packed full of delicious recipes that are nutritious and substantial, even the most discerning palate is sure to be satisfied.

Healthy Eating

Variety, of course, is the keynote to healthy eating, whatever the diet. As long as the day's meals contain a good mixture of different food types—carbohydrates, proteins and fats—a balanced diet and adequate supplies of essential vitamins and proteins are almost guaranteed. Typical dishes that are based on fresh vegetables, pulses, pasta, or rice also have the advantage of being low in fats, particularly saturated fats, and high in complex carbohydrates and fiber, resulting in a diet that is in tune with modern nutritional thinking.

Vegetables are an important source of vitamins, especially vitamin C. Green vegetables and pulses contain many B-group vitamins. Both carrots and dark green vegetables contain high levels of carotene, which is used by the body to manufacture vitamin A. Carrots also contain useful quantities of vitamins B3, C, and E. Vegetable oils contain vitamin E and most are also high in polyunsaturated fats. Vegetables are also a particularly good source of many essential minerals, especially calcium, iron, magnesium, and potassium.

There is a long and honorable tradition of the specific, health-giving properties of different vegetables, which dates back at least as far as the Middle Ages. These qualities, once dismissed as old wives' tales, are now being recognized and valued again. Onions and garlic, for example, contain cycloallin, an anticoagulant that helps protect against heart disease. Garlic also contains a strong antibiotic, is thought to protect the body against some major diseases, and also increases the absorption of many vitamins.

There is no question that a sensible vegetarian diet is at least as healthy as a sensible meat-eating diet and some nutritionists maintain that it is better. However, there are one or two particular points that are worth noting. Proteins are made up of "building blocks" called amino acids and, while all those essential to the human body are easily obtained from most animal products, they are not always present in many vegetarian foods. A good mixed diet will prevent this from being a problem. For example, legumes are an excellent source of protein, but

they do lack one essential amino acid called methionine. Grains, on the other hand, contain this amino acid, although they lack two others, tryptophan and lysine. A dish that contains both rice and beans, a plate of hummus and pitta bread, or a bowl of bean soup and a slice of wholemeal toast, for example, will ensure that all the necessary first-class proteins are available to the body.

Dairy products are also a valuable source of protein, but they are high in fat. It is very easy for busy people to fall into the habit of basing rather a lot of meals around cheese, for example, resulting in an unhealthily high intake of cholesterol. Eaten in moderation, however, cheese is a very useful and versatile ingredient in the vegetarian diet. If you do use dairy products a lot, it may be worth considering buying lowfat types, such as skim or semiskim milk, lowfat yogurt, and soft cheeses.

It is important to be aware that the body cannot absorb iron from vegetable sources unless vitamin C is ingested at the same meal. Although many vegetables also contain vitamin C, this is easily destroyed through cooking. Some raw fruit, a glass of fruit juice, or a side salad are simple and tasty solutions.

Vegans, who do not eat any dairy products, must be a little more scrupulous than straightforward vegetarians about ensuring that they obtain all the necessary nutrients. A lack of calcium, in particular, can be a problem, but this can be countered with a mineral supplement or by using calcium-enriched soy milk. A vegan diet may be just as healthy as a vegetarian or meat-eating one.

No foods can really be said to be bad for you, although some are best eaten in moderation. It is sensible to keep an eye on the quantities of butter, cream, high-fat cheeses, dried fruits, oils, and salted nuts that you eat each day. Other popular vegetarian ingredients, such as grains, vegetables, legumes, fruit, bread, pasta, and noodles can be eaten more freely. All diets should include raw vegetables and fruit and these should comprise as much as 40 percent of a vegetarian diet.

Finally, a hidden advantage to changing to a vegetarian diet is that, usually, it initially entails thinking in a more detailed way about all the things you eat. This may extend across the whole spectrum of nutrition, including such things as your intake of salt, sugar, and refined foods. As a result, many long-term vegetarians have developed eating patterns that are among the healthiest in the world.

Vegetables

Vegetables are, of course, at the heart of a vegetarian diet, offering an almost endless choice of flavors and textures. Preparing and cooking them with care makes sure that they may be enjoyed at their best and that they retain their full nutritional value.

Buying

The fresher vegetables are, the better. Nevertheless, some, such as root vegetables, can be stored for relatively long periods in a cool, dark place and most will keep for two or three days in the salad drawer of the refrigerator. Superstores are very convenient and carry a wide range of good-quality vegetables, and finding a really high-quality supplier—possibly of organically-grown vegetables—will be repaid many times over in terms of flavor and nutritional value.

Whatever type you are buying, always look for unblemished and undamaged vegetables with no discoloration. Greens should have a good color, with no wilting leaves, root vegetables should be firm and crisp, vegetable fruits, such as tomatoes and bell peppers, should not have soggy patches or wrinkled skin. No vegetables should ever look or smell stale.

Preparing

Use vegetables as soon after buying them as possible, but try not to prepare them much in advance of cooking. If they are left exposed to air or soaking in water, many vitamins and other valuable nutrients are leached out or destroyed.

The highest concentration of nutrients is in the layer directly under the skin, so if possible, avoid peeling them altogether. If they must be peeled, try to do it very thinly. A swivel vegetable peeler is a worthwhile investment. Also, consider cooking potatoes, for example, in their skins—first scrubbing off any soil or dirt—and peeling them afterwards. The skin comes off in a much thinner layer than when they are peeled raw.

How thickly or thinly vegetables are sliced, or how large or small they are chopped will depend, to some extent, on the method of cooking and the individual recipe instructions. However, remember that the smaller and finer the pieces, the greater the surface area from which nutrients can leach.

Green & Leafy Vegetables

Broccoli

Trim the stalk. Leave whole or break into flowerets—small "flowers" with a little stalk attached—according to the recipe. Wash thoroughly.

Brussels Sprouts

Trim the end of the stalk and remove the outer leaves.

Cabbage

Remove the outer leaves, if necessary, cut in fourths and cut out the stem. Slice or shred according to the recipe.

Cauliflower

Cut off the thick stalk, level with the base of the head, and cut out the core. Remove larger, coarse leaves, but smaller ones can be left. Leave the head whole or break into flowerets.

Chinese Cabbage

Remove the outer leaves and slice the quantity required.

Fava Beans

Top and tail and roughly slice very young beans that are less than 3 inches/7.5 cm long. Shell older beans and, if wished, skin after cooking.

Green Beans

Top and tail young beans with kitchen scissors or a knife and leave whole. Snap off the ends of older beans and pull off any strings. Slice diagonally or shred before cooking.

Kale & Curly Kale

Break the leaves from the stalk, cut out thick stalks and cook whole or shredded.

Peas

Pop the fat end of the pod, split open and remove the peas.

Pole Beans

Top, tail and string, then slice lengthwise, not diagonally.

Snow Peas & Sugar Snap Peas

Top and tail, then leave whole.

Spinach

Rinse gently, but thoroughly, in two changes of cold water. Pull or cut off tough stalks.

Shoots and Stems

Asparagus

Trim the woody end of the stalk. White asparagus stems usually require peeling.

Celery

Trim the base and separate the stalks. Wash thoroughly and slice thickly or thinly. If using raw in a salad, pull off any coarse strings.

Fennel

Remove the outer layer of skin, except from very young bulbs. Slice downward or horizontally according to the recipe. Use the fronds for a garnish.

Globe Artichokes

Twist off the stem and cut the base flat, removing any small, spiky leaves. Cut off the top 1/3 inch/1 cm and trim the points of the remaining leaves.

Root Vegetables

Carrots

Trim the ends and scrub young carrots, as they do not need peeling. They may be left whole, sliced, or diced. Thinly peel older carrots and, if necessary, cut out the woody core.

Celery Root

Peel off the thick skin immediately before cooking, as the flesh quickly discolors. Slice or chop according to the recipe. If necessary, put the pieces into a bowl of water acidulated with a little lemon juice.

Jerusalem Artichokes

Scrub in cold water and cook in their skins before peeling. Otherwise peel immediately before use, placing them in water acidulated with a little lemon juice to prevent discoloration.

Leeks

Trim the root and the dark leaves. Cut in half lengthwise or prepare according to the recipe and wash well in plenty of cold water. Drain thoroughly.

Onions & Shallots

Peel off the papery skin, trim and slice or chop according to the recipe.

Parsnips

Trim and thinly peel. Small parsnips may be left whole, but older parsnips may be halved, sliced or diced according to the recipe.

Potatoes

Wash new potatoes in cold running water and cook in their skins. Scrub old potatoes and either cook in their skins, depending on the method, and peel afterwards, or thinly peel before cooking.

Rutabagas

Peel off the thick skin. Chop or dice according to the recipe.

Scallions

Trim the root and cut off any wilted green leaves. Slice or chop according to the recipe.

Sweet Potatoes

Scrub and cook in their skins and peel afterward or thinly peel and put in water acidulated with lemon juice.

Salad Vegetables

Arugula

Discard any discolored leaves and wash the remainder.

Belgian Endive

Using a sharp, pointed knife, remove the core from the base. Discard any wilted leaves, then wash and dry thoroughly.

Cucumbers

Wash and peel, if liked. Always peel glossy, waxed cucumbers. Slice thinly or dice for salads. If cooking cucumber, first cut into wedges and remove the seeds.

Escarole

Separate the leaves and discard any that are discolored. Wash thoroughly and pat dry.

Lettuce

Separate the leaves and wash in several changes of water. Adding vinegar to the first rinse will kill any insects in lettuces grown outdoors. Spin or wrap in a clean dish towel and shake dry. Tear loose-leafed lettuces into smaller pieces and slice or shred firm lettuce.

Mooli

Trim and wash, then slice, dice, or grate, according to the recipe.

Radicchio

Separate the leaves and discard any that are discolored. Wash thoroughly and pat dry with a clean dish towel.

or dice in the shells and then scoop out the diced flesh.

Bell Peppers

For stuffing, cut a slice from the top, cut out the inner core and shake out any remaining seeds. For other dishes, halve and remove the core and seeds, then cut into fourths, slice, or dice. To peel bell peppers, cut into halves or fourths and broil, skin side up, until charred and beginning to blister. Transfer the pieces of bell pepper to a plastic bag, seal and set aside for 5–10 minutes. The skin will peel easily.

Eggplants

Newer varieties no longer require salting to remove the bitter taste; they are not so bitter as older varieties. However, salting still helps to draw out some of the moisture. Wash the eggplant, cut into slices or segments, according to the recipe, place in a colander and sprinkle generously with salt. Leave for 30 minutes, rinse well and pat dry with paper towels.

Tomatoes

Wash well. To peel, cut a cross in the skin at the base, briefly blanch in boiling water and rinse in cold water. The skin should then peel off easily. Cut salad tomatoes and those for pizza toppings horizontally. Slice others according to the recipe.

Radishes

Wash and leave whole or slice.

Watercress

Discard any wilted or discolored leaves and remove any thick stalks. Wash thoroughly.

Squashes

Pumpkins

Peel and chop.

Summer Squashes

Wash, then peel if the skin is tough or if the vegetable is to be braised or sautéed.

Zucchini

Leave tiny, baby zucchini whole – with their flowers. Top and tail, then slice, dice or stuff larger zucchini, according to the recipe.

Vegetable Fruits

Avocados

Halve and remove the stone, then sprinkle the flesh with lemon juice to prevent discoloration. Leave in halves for serving with a vinaigrette. For other dishes, slice and then peel,

How to Use This Book

Each recipe contains a wealth of useful information, including a breakdown of nutritional quantities, preparation and cooking times, and level of difficulty. All of this information is explained in detail below.

A full-color photograph of the finished dish.

The ingredients for each recipe are listed in the order that they are used.

The nutritional information provided for each recipe is per serving or per portion. Optional ingredients, variations or serving suggestions have not been included in the calculations.

The method is clearly explained with step-by-step instructions that are easy to follow.

Cook's tips provide useful information regarding ingredients or cooking techniques.

15

VEGETARIAN

A wonderful mixture of red lentils, bean curd, and vegetables is cooked beneath a crunchy potato topping for a really hearty meal.

Potato-Topped Lentil Bake

SERVES 4

topping
4½ cups diced mealy potatoes
2 tbsp butter
1 tbsp milk
½ cup chopped pecan nuts
2 tbsp chopped fresh thyme
thyme sprigs, to garnish

filling
1¼ cups red lentils, washed
¼ cup butter
1 leek, sliced
2 garlic cloves, crushed
1 celery stalk, chopped
1¼ cups broccoli flowerets
6 oz/175 g smoked bean curd, cubed
2 tsp tomato paste
salt and pepper

1 To make the topping, cook the diced potatoes in a pan of boiling water for 10–15 minutes, or until cooked through. Drain well, add the butter and milk, and mash thoroughly. Stir in the chopped pecan nuts and the chopped thyme and set aside.

2 Cook the lentils in boiling water for 20–30 minutes, or until tender. Drain and set aside.

3 Melt the butter in a skillet. Add the leek, garlic, celery, and broccoli. Fry over medium heat, stirring frequently, for 5 minutes, until soft.

4 Add the bean curd cubes. Stir in the lentils, together with the tomato paste. Season with salt and pepper to taste, then turn the mixture into the base of a shallow ovenproof dish.

5 Spoon the mashed potato on top of the lentil mixture, spreading to cover it completely.

6 Cook the lentil bake in a preheated oven, 400°F/200°C, for about 30–35 minutes, or until the topping is golden brown. Remove the bake from the oven, garnish with sprigs of fresh thyme, and serve hot.

NUTRITION
Calories 627; Sugars 7 g; Protein 26 g; Carbohydrate 66 g; Fat 30 g; Saturates 13 g

⊛⊛⊛ moderate
🕐 10 mins
🕐 1 hr 30 mins

🍳 COOK'S TIP

You can use almost any combination of your favorite vegetables in this dish.

⭐ The number of stars represents the difficulty of each recipe, ranging from very easy (1 star) to challenging (4 stars).

🕐 This amount of time represents the preparation of ingredients, including cooling, chilling and soaking times.

🕐 This represents the cooking time.

Basic Recipes

These recipes form the basis of several of the dishes contained in this book. Many of these basic recipes can be made in advance and stored in the refrigerator until required.

Fresh Vegetable Bouillon

8 oz/225 g shallots
1 large carrot, diced
1 celery stalk, chopped
½ fennel bulb
1 garlic clove
1 bay leaf
a few fresh parsley and tarragon sprigs
8 cups water
pepper

1 Put all of the ingredients in a large saucepan and bring to a boil. Skim off the surface scum with a flat spoon and reduce to a gentle simmer. Partially cover and cook for 45 minutes. Leave to cool.

2 Line a strainer with clean cheesecloth and put over a large pitcher or bowl. Pour the bouillon through the strainer. Discard the herbs and vegetables. Cover and store in small quantities in the refrigerator for up to 3 days.

Béchamel Sauce

2½ cups milk
4 whole cloves
1 bay leaf
pinch of freshly grated nutmeg
2 tbsp butter or margarine
2 tbsp all-purpose flour
salt and pepper

1 Put the milk in a saucepan and add the cloves, bay leaf, and nutmeg. Gradually bring to a boil. Remove from the heat and leave for 15 minutes.

2 Melt the butter or margarine in another saucepan and stir in the flour to make a roux. Cook, stirring, for 1 minute. Remove the pan from the heat.

3 Strain the milk and gradually blend into the roux. Return the pan to the heat and bring to the boil, stirring, until the sauce thickens. Season with salt and pepper to taste and add any flavorings.

Tahini Cream

3 tbsp tahini (sesame seed paste)
6 tbsp water
2 tsp lemon juice
1 garlic clove, crushed
salt and pepper

1 Blend together the tahini and water.

2 Stir in the lemon juice and garlic. Season with salt and pepper to taste. The tahini cream is now ready to serve.

Tomato Sauce

2 tbsp olive oil
1 small onion, chopped
1 garlic clove, crushed
14 oz /400 g canned tomatoes
1 tbsp chopped fresh basil
1 bay leaf
2 tbsp tomato purée
2 tsp sugar
salt and pepper

1 Heat the oil in a pan. Fry the onion until translucent. Add the garlic and cook for another minute.

2 Stir in the tomatoes, basil, bay leaf, tomato purée, and sugar, and season to taste.

3 Bring to the boil, reduce the heat and simmer for 15–20 minutes or until reduced by half. Discard the bay leaf and adjust the seasoning.

Green Herb Dressing

¼ cup fresh parsley
¼ cup fresh mint
¼ cup fresh chives
1 garlic clove, crushed
⅔ cup plain yogurt
salt and pepper

1 Remove the stalks from the parsley and mint and put the leaves in a blender or food processor.

2 Add the chives, garlic, and yogurt and salt and pepper to taste. Blend until smooth, then store in the refrigerator until needed.

Sesame Dressing

2 tbsp tahini (sesame seed paste)
2 tbsp cider vinegar
2 tbsp medium sherry
2 tbsp sesame oil
1 tbsp soy sauce
1 garlic clove, crushed

1 Put the tahini in a bowl and gradually mix in the vinegar and sherry until smooth. Add the sesame oil, soy sauce, and garlic and mix together thoroughly.

Cucumber Dressing

scant 1 cup plain yogurt
2-inch/5-cm piece of cucumber, peeled
1 tbsp chopped fresh mint leaves
½ tsp grated lemon peel
pinch of superfine sugar
salt and pepper

1 Put the yogurt, cucumber, mint, lemon peel, sugar, and salt and pepper to taste in a blender or food processor and work until smooth. Alternatively, finely chop the cucumber and combine with the other ingredients. Serve chilled.

Apple and Cider Vinegar Dressing

2 tbsp sunflower oil
2 tbsp concentrated apple juice
2 tbsp cider vinegar
1 tbsp Meaux mustard
1 garlic clove, crushed
salt and pepper

1 Put the oil, apple juice, cider vinegar, mustard, garlic, and salt and pepper to taste in a screw-top jar and shake vigorously until well-mixed.

Warm Walnut Dressing

6 tbsp walnut oil
3 tbsp white wine vinegar
1 tbsp clear honey
1 tsp wholegrain mustard
1 garlic clove, sliced
salt and pepper

1 Put the oil, vinegar, honey, mustard, and salt and pepper to taste in a saucepan and whisk together.

2 Add the garlic and heat very gently for 3 minutes. Remove the garlic slices with a draining spoon and discard. Pour the dressing over the salad and serve immediately.

Tomato Dressing

½ cup tomato juice
1 garlic clove, crushed
2 tbsp lemon juice
1 tbsp soy sauce
1 tsp clear honey
2 tbsp chopped fresh chives
salt and pepper

1 Put the tomato juice, garlic, lemon juice, soy sauce, honey, chives, and salt and pepper to taste in a screw-top jar and shake vigorously until well-mixed.

Soups

Soup is easy to make, but always produces delicious results. There is an enormous variety of soups that you can make with vegetables. They can be rich and creamy, thick and chunky, light and delicate, and hot or chilled. The vegetables are often puréed to give a smooth consistency and thicken the soup, but you can also purée just some of the mixture to give the soup more texture and interest. A wide range of ingredients can be used in addition to vegetables—legumes, grains, noodles, cheese, and yogurt all work well. You can also experiment with different substitutions if you don't have certain ingredients to hand. Whatever your preference, you're sure to enjoy the variety of tasty soups contained in this chapter. Serve with fresh, crusty bread for a truly delicious meal.

A thick vegetable soup which is a delicious meal in itself. Serve the soup with thin shavings of Parmesan and warm ciabatta bread.

Winter Soup

SERVES 4

2 tbsp olive oil
2 leeks, thinly sliced
2 zucchini, chopped
2 garlic cloves, crushed
4 cups canned chopped tomatoes
1 tbsp tomato paste
1 bay leaf
3½ cups Fresh Vegetable Bouillon (see page 16)
3½ cups canned garbanzo beans, drained
8 oz/225 g spinach
1 oz/25 g Parmesan cheese, thinly shaved
salt and pepper
crusty bread, to serve

1 Heat the oil in a heavy pan. Add the sliced leeks and zucchini and cook over medium heat, stirring constantly, for 5 minutes.

2 Add the garlic, chopped tomatoes, tomato paste, bay leaf, vegetable bouillon, and garbanzo beans. Bring to a boil, lower the heat, and simmer, stirring occasionally, for 5 minutes.

3 Shred the spinach finely and add it to the soup. Cook the soup for a further 2 minutes over medium-high heat, until the spinach is just wilted. Season to taste with salt and pepper.

4 Remove the bay leaf. Pour the soup into a warmed tureen or individual bowls and sprinkle over the Parmesan. Serve with crusty bread.

NUTRITION
Calories 285; Sugars 11 g; Protein 16 g;
Carbohydrate 29 g; Fat 12 g; Saturates 3 g

very easy

10 mins

20 mins

Homemade tomato soup is easy to make and often tastes better than bought varieties. Try this version with its Mediterranean influences.

Plum Tomato Soup

1 Heat the oil in a large pan. Add the onions, celery, and carrot and cook over low heat, stirring frequently, until soft, but not colored.

2 Add the tomatoes, bouillon, chopped herbs, wine, and sugar. Bring to a boil, cover, and simmer for 20 minutes.

3 Place the toasted hazelnuts in a blender or food processor, together with the olives and basil leaves, and process until thoroughly combined, but not too smooth. Alternatively, finely chop the nuts, olives, and basil leaves, and pound them together in a mortar with a pestle, then turn into a small bowl. Add the olive oil and process or beat thoroughly for a few seconds to combine. Turn the mixture into a serving bowl.

4 Meanwhile, warm the ciabatta bread in a preheated oven, 375°F/190°C, for 3–4 minutes.

5 Process the soup in a blender or a food processor, or press through a strainer, until smooth. Check the seasoning. Ladle into warmed soup bowls and garnish with basil sprigs. Slice the warm bread and spread with the olive and hazelnut paste. Serve with the soup.

S E R V E S   4

2 tbsp olive oil
2 red onions, chopped
2 celery stalks, chopped
1 carrot, chopped
1 lb/450 g plum tomatoes, halved
3 cups Fresh Vegetable Bouillon
   (see page 16)
1 tbsp chopped fresh oregano
1 tbsp chopped fresh basil
²⁄₃ cups dry white wine
2 tsp superfine sugar
1 cup hazelnuts, toasted
1 cups black or green olives
handful of fresh basil leaves
1 tbsp olive oil
1 loaf ciabatta bread
salt and pepper
fresh basil sprigs to garnish

N U T R I T I O N
Calories *402*; Sugars *14 g*; Protein *7 g*;
Carbohydrate *16 g*; Fat *32 g*; Saturates *3 g*

very easy

20 mins

30–35 mins

This Spanish soup is full of chopped and grated vegetables with a puréed tomato base. It requires chilling, so prepare well in advance.

Gazpacho

SERVES 4

½ small cucumber
½ small green bell pepper, halved, seeded, and very finely chopped
1 lb/450 g ripe tomatoes, peeled or 2 cups canned chopped tomatoes
½ onion, coarsely chopped
2–3 garlic cloves, crushed
3 tbsp olive oil
2 tbsp white wine vinegar
1–2 tbsp lemon or lime juice
2 tbsp tomato paste
1¾ cups tomato juice
salt and pepper

to serve

chopped green bell pepper
thinly sliced onion rings
garlic croûtons

NUTRITION

Calories *140*; Sugars *12 g*; Protein *3 g*;
Carbohydrate *13 g*; Fat *9 g*; Saturates *1 g*

⭐ very easy
🍲 6 hrs 30 mins
🕐 0 mins

1 Coarsely grate the cucumber into a large bowl and add the chopped green bell pepper.

2 Put the tomatoes, onion, and garlic in a food processor or blender, add the oil, vinegar, lemon juice, and tomato paste and process until a smooth purée is formed. Alternatively, finely chop the tomatoes and finely grate the onion, then mix together and add the crushed garlic, oil, vinegar, lemon juice, and tomato paste.

3 Add the tomato mixture to the bowl and mix well, then add the tomato juice and mix again.

4 Season to taste, cover the bowl with plastic wrap, and chill thoroughly—for at least 6 hours and preferably longer, so that the flavors have time to blend.

5 Prepare the side dishes of chopped green bell pepper, thinly sliced onion rings, and garlic croûtons and arrange them in individual serving bowls.

6 Ladle the soup into chilled bowls, preferably from a soup tureen set in the center of the table with the side dishes of bell pepper, onion rings, and croûtons placed around it. Hand the dishes round to allow the guests to help themselves.

This American classic has now become popular worldwide. When pumpkin is out of season, use butternut squash in its place.

Pumpkin Soup

1 Peel the pumpkin, remove the seeds, and then cut the flesh into 1-inch/ 2.5-cm cubes.

2 Melt the butter or margarine in a large, heavy pan. Add the onion and garlic and cook over low heat until soft, but not colored.

3 Add the pumpkin and toss with the onion for 2–3 minutes.

4 Add the bouillon and bring to a boil over medium heat. Season to taste with salt and pepper and add the ground ginger and lemon juice, the strips of orange peel, if using, and the bay leaves or bouquet garni.

5 Cover the pan and gently simmer the soup over low heat for about 20 minutes, stirring occasionally, until the pumpkin is tender.

6 Discard the orange peel, if using, and the bay leaves or bouquet garni. Cool the soup slightly, then press through a strainer with the back of a spoon, or process in a food processor until smooth. Pour into a clean pan.

7 Add the milk and reheat gently. Adjust the seasoning. Garnish with a swirl of cream or plain yogurt and snipped chives, and serve.

SERVES 6

about 2 lb/900 g pumpkin
3 tbsp butter or margarine
1 onion, thinly sliced
1 garlic clove, crushed
3½ cups Fresh Vegetable Bouillon
    (see page 16)
½ tsp ground ginger
1 tbsp lemon juice
3–4 thinly pared strips of
    orange peel (optional)
1–2 bay leaves or 1 bouquet garni
1¼ cups milk
salt and pepper

to garnish
4–6 tbsp light or heavy cream
    or plain yogurt
snipped fresh chives

NUTRITION
Calories *112*; Sugars *7 g*; Protein *4 g*;
Carbohydrate *8 g*; Fat *7 g*; Saturates *2 g*

very easy

10 mins

30 mins

This soup has a real Mediterranean flavor, using sweet red bell peppers, tomato, chile, and basil. It is great served with olive bread.

Pepper *and* Chile Soup

SERVES 4

1/2 lb/225 g red bell peppers, halved, seeded and sliced
1 onion, sliced
2 garlic cloves, crushed
1 fresh green chile, chopped
1 1/4 cups crushed tomatoes
2 1/2 cups Fresh Vegetable Bouillon (see page 16)
2 tbsp chopped fresh basil
fresh basil sprigs, to garnish

1 Put the red bell peppers in a large pan with the onion, garlic, and chile. Add the crushed tomatoes and the vegetable bouillon and bring to a boil, stirring well.

2 Reduce the heat to a simmer and continue to cook the vegetables for 20 minutes, or until the bell peppers are soft. Drain, reserving the liquid and vegetables separately.

3 Using the back of a spoon, press the vegetables through a strainer. Alternatively, process in a food processor until smooth.

4 Return the vegetable purée to a clean pan with the reserved cooking liquid. Add the basil and heat through until hot. Garnish the soup with fresh basil sprigs and serve immediately.

NUTRITION
Calories 55; Sugars 10 g; Protein 2 g;
Carbohydrate 11 g; Fat 0.5 g; Saturates 0.1 g

⊗ very easy
◔ 10 mins
◷ 25 mins

🍳 **COOK'S TIP**

This soup is also delicious served cold with 2/3 cup plain yogurt swirled into it.

This is a classic combination of ingredients all brought together in a delicious, creamy soup. Serve with whole-wheat bread for a light lunch.

Stilton *and* Walnut Soup

1 Melt the butter in a large, heavy pan and sauté the shallots, celery, and garlic for 2–3 minutes, stirring, until soft.

2 Lower the heat, add the flour and cook, stirring, for 30 seconds.

3 Gradually stir in the vegetable bouillon and milk and bring to a boil.

4 Reduce the heat to a simmer and add the crumbled blue Stilton cheese and walnut halves. Cover and simmer for 20 minutes.

5 Stir the plain yogurt into the soup and heat for a further 2 minutes without boiling.

6 Season the soup, then transfer to a warm soup tureen or individual serving bowls,

7 Garnish the soup with the chopped celery leaves and extra crumbled blue Stilton cheese, and serve immediately.

SERVES 4

4 tbsp butter
2 shallots, chopped
3 celery stalks, chopped
1 garlic clove, finely chopped
2 tbsp all-purpose flour
2½ cups Fresh Vegetable Bouillon (see page 16)
1¼ cups milk
1½ cups crumbled blue Stilton cheese, plus extra to garnish
2 tbsp walnut halves, roughly chopped
²⁄₃ cup plain yogurt
salt and pepper
chopped celery leaves, to garnish

NUTRITION
Calories *392*; Sugars *8 g*; Protein *15 g*;
Carbohydrate 15 *g*; Fat *30 g*; Saturates *16 g*

⭐⭐⭐   moderate
🕐   15 mins
🕐   20 mins

🧑‍🍳 **COOK'S TIP**

As well as adding protein, vitamins, and useful fats to the diet, nuts add important flavor and texture to vegetarian meals.

A delicious creamy soup with grated carrot and parsley for texture and color. Serve with crusty cheese biscuits for a hearty lunch.

Thick Onion Soup

SERVES 4

1/3 cup butter
1 lb/450 g onions, finely chopped
1 garlic clove, crushed
1/3 cup all-purpose flour
2 1/2 cups Fresh Vegetable Bouillon
    (see page 16)
2 1/2 cups milk
2–3 tsp lemon or lime juice
good pinch of ground allspice
1 bay leaf
1 carrot, coarsely grated
4–6 tbsp heavy cream
salt and pepper
2 tbsp chopped fresh parsley, to garnish

cheese biscuits

1 1/3 cups malted wheat or whole-wheat flour
2 tsp baking powder
1/4 cup butter
4 tbsp grated Parmesan cheese
1 egg, beaten
about 1/3 cup milk

NUTRITION

Calories *277*; Sugars *12 g*; Protein *6 g*;
Carbohydrate *19 g*; Fat *20 g*; Saturates *8 g*

easy

20 mins

1 hr 10 mins

1 Melt the butter in a pan and cook the onions and garlic over low heat, stirring frequently, for 10–15 minutes, until soft, but not colored. Stir in the flour and cook, stirring, for 1 minute, then gradually stir in the bouillon and bring to a boil, stirring frequently. Add the milk, then bring back to a boil.

2 Season to taste with salt and pepper and add 2 teaspoons of the lemon juice, the allspice, and the bay leaf. Cover and simmer for about 25 minutes until the vegetables are tender. Discard the bay leaf.

3 Meanwhile, make the biscuits. Combine the flour, baking powder, and seasoning and rub in the butter until the mixture resembles fine bread crumbs. Stir in 3 tablespoons of the cheese, the egg, and enough milk to mix to a soft dough.

4 Shape into a bar about 3/4-inch/2-cm thick. Place on a floured cookie sheet and mark into slices. Sprinkle with the remaining cheese and bake in a preheated oven, 425°F/220°C, for about 20 minutes, until risen and a golden brown color.

5 Stir the carrot into the soup and simmer for 2–3 minutes. Add more lemon juice, if necessary. Stir in the cream and reheat. Garnish with parsley and serve with the warm biscuits.

Parsnips make a delicious soup as they have a slightly sweet flavor. In this recipe, spices are added to complement this sweetness.

Curried Parsnip Soup

1 Heat the vegetable oil and butter in a large pan until the butter has melted. Add the onion, parsnips, and garlic and sauté, stirring frequently, for about 5–7 minutes, until the vegetables are soft, but not colored.

2 Add the garam masala and chili powder and cook, stirring constantly, for 30 seconds. Sprinkle in the flour, mixing well, and cook, stirring constantly, for a further 30 seconds.

3 Stir in the bouillon, lemon peel, and lemon juice and bring to a boil. Reduce the heat and simmer for 20 minutes.

4 Remove some of the vegetable pieces with a slotted spoon and reserve until required. Transfer the remaining soup and vegetables to a food processor or blender and process for about 1 minute, or until a smooth purée is formed. Alternatively, press the vegetables through a strainer with the back of a wooden spoon.

5 Return the soup to a clean pan and stir in the reserved vegetables. Heat the soup through for 2 minutes until piping hot.

6 Season to taste with salt and pepper, then transfer to soup bowls, garnish with grated lemon peel, and serve.

SERVES 4

1 tbsp vegetable oil
1 tbsp butter
1 red onion, chopped
3 parsnips, chopped
2 garlic cloves, crushed
2 tsp garam masala
½ tsp chili powder
1 tbsp all-purpose flour
3½ cups Fresh Vegetable Bouillon (see page 16)
grated peel and juice of 1 lemon
salt and pepper
lemon peel, to garnish

NUTRITION
Calories *152*; Sugars *7 g*; Protein *3 g*; Carbohydrate *18 g*; Fat *8 g*; Saturates *3 g*

⭐   very easy

🕐   10 mins

🕐   35 mins

Spinach is the basis for this delicious soup, which has creamy mascarpone cheese stirred through it to give it a wonderful texture.

Spinach *and* Mascarpone Soup

SERVES 4

4 tbsp butter
1 bunch scallions, trimmed and chopped
2 celery stalks, chopped
3/4 lb/350 g spinach or sorrel, or
   3 bunches watercress
3 1/2 cups Fresh Vegetable Bouillon
   (see page 16)
1 x 8 oz/225 g tub mascarpone cheese
1 tbsp olive oil
2 slices thick-cut bread, cut into cubes
1/2 tsp caraway seeds
salt and pepper
sesame bread sticks, to serve

1 Melt half the butter in a very large pan. Add the scallions and celery, and cook over medium heat, stirring frequently, for about 5 minutes, until soft.

2 Pack the spinach, into the pan. Add the vegetable bouillon and bring to a boil, then reduce the heat, cover, and simmer for about 15–20 minutes.

3 Transfer the soup to a blender or food processor and process until smooth. Alternatively, rub it through a strainer. Return to the pan.

4 Add the mascarpone to the soup and heat gently, stirring constantly, until smooth and blended. Season to taste with salt and pepper.

5 Heat the remaining butter with the olive oil in a skillet. Add the bread cubes and fry, turning frequently, until golden brown, adding the caraway seeds toward the end of cooking, so that they do not burn.

6 Ladle the soup into warmed bowls. Sprinkle with the croûtons and serve with the sesame bread sticks.

NUTRITION
Calories *402*; Sugars *2 g*; Protein *11 g*;
Carbohydrate *10 g*; Fat *36 g*; Saturates *21 g*

⭐   very easy

🕐   15 mins

🕐   30 mins

COOK'S TIP

Any leafy vegetable can be used to vary the flavor of this soup. For anyone who grows their own vegetables, it is the perfect recipe for experimenting with a glut of produce. Try young beet leaves or surplus lettuces for a change.

A quick, chunky soup, ideal for a snack or a quick lunch. Save some of the soup and purée it to make one portion of creamed soup for the next day.

Leek, Potato, *and* Carrot Soup

1 Trim off and discard some of the coarse green part of the leek, then slice thinly and rinse thoroughly in cold water. Drain well.

2 Heat the sunflower oil in a heavy pan. Add the leek and garlic and cook over low heat for about 2–3 minutes, until soft, but barely colored. Add the bouillon, bay leaf, and cumin and season to taste. Bring to a boil, stirring constantly.

3 Add the diced potato to the pan, cover, and simmer over low heat for 10–15 minutes. Keep a careful eye on the soup during the cooking time to make sure the potato cooks until it is just tender, but not broken up.

4 Add the grated carrot to the pan and simmer the soup for a further 2–3 minutes. Adjust the seasoning if necessary, discard the bay leaf, and serve the soup in warmed bowls, sprinkled liberally with the chopped parsley.

5 To make a puréed soup, first process the leftovers (about half the original soup) in a blender or food processor until smooth, or press through a strainer with the back of a wooden spoon, and then return to a clean pan. Add the milk to the pan, bring the soup to a boil, and simmer for 2–3 minutes.

6 Adjust the seasoning and stir in the heavy cream, or sour cream before serving the soup in warmed bowls, sprinkled with chopped parsley.

SERVES 2

1 leek, about 6 oz/175 g
1 tbsp sunflower oil
1 garlic clove, crushed
3 cups Fresh Vegetable Bouillon (see page 16)
1 bay leaf
1/4 tsp ground cumin
1 1/2 cups diced potatoes
generous 1/2 cup coarsely grated carrot
salt and pepper
chopped fresh parsley, to garnish

pureed soup
5–6 tbsp milk
1–2 tbsp heavy cream, or sour cream

NUTRITION
Calories *156*; Sugars *7 g*; Protein *4 g*; Carbohydrate *22 g*; Fat *6 g*; Saturates *0.7g*

⭐ very easy
🍽 10 mins
🕐 25 mins

This creamy soup has a delightful pale green coloring and rich flavor from the blend of tender broccoli and blue cheese.

Broccoli *and* Potato Soup

SERVES 4

2 tbsp olive oil
2²/₃ cups diced potatoes
1 onion, diced
2 cups broccoli flowerets
1 cup crumbled blue cheese
4¹/₂ cups Fresh Vegetable Bouillon
   (see page 16)
²/₃ cup heavy cream
pinch of paprika
salt and pepper

1 Heat the oil in a large pan and add the diced potatoes and onion. Sauté gently for 5 minutes, stirring constantly.

2 Reserve a few broccoli flowerets for the garnish and add the remaining broccoli to the pan. Add the crumbled blue cheese and bouillon.

3 Bring to a boil, then reduce the heat, cover the pan, and simmer for 25 minutes, until the potatoes are tender.

4 Transfer the soup to a food processor or blender in batches and process until the mixture is a smooth purée.

5 Return the purée to a clean pan and stir in the cream and a pinch of paprika. Season to taste.

6 Blanch the reserved broccoli flowerets in a little boiling water for approximately 2 minutes, then drain with a slotted spoon.

7 Pour the soup into warmed bowls and garnish with the broccoli flowerets and a sprinkling of paprika. Serve immediately.

NUTRITION
Calories *452*; Sugars *4 g*; Protein *14 g*;
Carbohydrate *20 g*; Fat *35 g*; Saturates *19 g*

moderate

5–10 mins

35 mins

🍳 **COOK'S TIP**

This soup freezes very successfully. Follow the method described here up to step 4, and freeze the soup after it has been puréed. Add the cream and paprika just before serving. Garnish and serve.

A slightly hot and spicy Indian flavor is given to this soup with the use of garam masala, chile, cumin, and cilantro.

Indian Potato *and* Pea Soup

1 Heat the vegetable oil in a large pan and add the diced potatoes, onion, and garlic. Sauté gently for about 5 minutes, stirring constantly.

2 Add the garam masala, ground coriander, and ground cumin, and cook for 1 minute, stirring all the time.

3 Stir in the vegetable bouillon and chopped red chile and bring the mixture to a boil. Reduce the heat, then cover the pan and simmer for 20 minutes, until the potatoes begin to break down.

4 Add the peas and cook for a further 5 minutes. Stir in the yogurt and season to taste with salt and pepper.

5 Pour into warmed soup bowls. Garnish with chopped fresh cilantro and serve hot with warm bread.

SERVES 4

2 tbsp vegetable oil
1¼ cups diced mealy potatoes
1 large onion, chopped
2 garlic cloves, crushed
1 tsp garam masala
1 tsp ground coriander
1 tsp ground cumin
3¾ cups Fresh Vegetable Bouillon (see page 16)
1 red chile, chopped
¾ cup frozen peas
4 tbsp plain yogurt
salt and pepper
chopped fresh cilantro, to garnish
warm bread, to serve

NUTRITION
Calories *153*; Sugars *6 g*; Protein *6 g*; Carbohydrate *18 g*; Fat *6 g*; Saturates *1 g*

★★★   moderate
🕐   15 mins
🕐   20 mins

🍳 COOK'S TIP

For slightly less heat, seed the chile before adding it to the soup. Always wash your hands after handling chiles because they contain volatile oils that can irritate the skin and make your eyes burn if you touch your face.

Fresh asparagus is now available for most of the year, so this soup can be made at any time. It can also be made using canned asparagus.

Asparagus Soup

SERVES 6

1 bunch asparagus, about 12 oz/350 g, or 2 packs mini asparagus, about 5½ oz/150 g each
3 cups Fresh Vegetable Bouillon (see page 16)
¼ cup butter or margarine
1 onion, chopped
3 tbsp all-purpose flour
¼ tsp ground coriander
1 tbsp lemon juice
2 cups milk
4–6 tbsp heavy or light cream
salt and pepper

1 Wash and trim the asparagus, discarding the lower, woody part of the stem. Cut the remainder into short lengths, keeping aside a few tips to use as a garnish. Mini asparagus does not need to be trimmed.

2 Cook the tips in the minimum of boiling salted water for 5–10 minutes. Drain and set aside.

3 Put the asparagus in a pan with the bouillon, bring to a boil, cover, and simmer for about 20 minutes, until soft. Drain and reserve the bouillon.

4 Melt the butter in a pan. Add the onion and cook over low heat until soft, but only barely colored. Stir in the flour and cook for 1 minute, then gradually whisk in the reserved bouillon, and bring to a boil.

5 Simmer for 2–3 minutes, until thickened, then stir in the cooked asparagus, seasoning, coriander, and lemon juice. Simmer for 10 minutes, then cool a little, and either press through a strainer with the back of a spoon or process in a blender or food processor until smooth.

6 Pour into a clean pan, add the milk and reserved asparagus tips, and bring to a boil. Simmer for 2 minutes. Stir in the cream, reheat gently, and serve.

NUTRITION

Calories *196*; Sugars *7 g*; Protein *7 g*; Carbohydrate *15 g*; Fat *12 g*; Saturates *4 g*

⭐ very easy

◔ 5–10 mins

🕐 55 mins

👨‍🍳 COOK'S TIP

If using canned asparagus, drain off the liquid and use as part of the measured bouillon. Remove a few small asparagus tips for garnish and chop the remainder. Continue from step 3.

Avocado has a rich flavor and color which makes a creamy flavored soup. It is best served chilled, but may be eaten warm.

Avocado *and* Vegetable Soup

1 Peel the avocado and mash the flesh with a fork, stir in the lemon juice, and reserve until required.

2 Heat the vegetable oil in a large pan. Add the corn, tomatoes, garlic, leek, and chile and sauté over low heat for 2–3 minutes, or until the vegetables are softened.

3 Put half the vegetable mixture in a food processor or blender, together with the mashed avocado, and process until smooth. Transfer the mixture to a clean pan.

4 Add the vegetable bouillon, milk, and reserved vegetables and cook over a low heat for 3–4 minutes, until hot.

5 Transfer to warmed individual serving bowls, garnish with shredded leek, and serve immediately.

S E R V E S 4

1 large, ripe avocado
2 tbsp lemon juice
1 tbsp vegetable oil
2 tbsp canned corn kernels, drained
2 tomatoes, peeled and seeded
1 garlic clove, crushed
1 leek, chopped
1 fresh red chile, chopped
1¾ cups Fresh Vegetable Bouillon (see page 16)
⅔ cup milk
shredded leek, to garnish

N U T R I T I O N
Calories *167*; Sugars *5 g*; Protein *4 g*;
Carbohydrate *8 g*; Fat *13 g*; Saturates *3 g*

⭐   very easy

🕒   15 mins

🕐   10 mins

👨‍🍳 **COOK'S TIP**

If serving chilled, transfer from the food processor to a bowl, stir in the vegetable bouillon and milk, cover, and chill in the refrigerator for at least 4 hours.

This is a classic creamy soup made from potatoes and leeks. To achieve the delicate pale color, be sure to use only the white parts of the leeks.

Vichyssoise

SERVES 6

3 large leeks
3 tbsp butter or margarine
1 onion, thinly sliced
1 lb/450 g potatoes, chopped
3½ cups Fresh Vegetable Bouillon (see page 16)
2 tsp lemon juice
pinch of ground nutmeg
¼ tsp ground coriander
1 bay leaf
1 egg yolk
⅔ cup light cream
salt and white pepper
freshly snipped chives, to garnish

1 Trim the leeks and remove most of the green part. Slice the white part of the leeks very finely.

2 Melt the butter in a pan. Add the leeks and onion and sauté, stirring occasionally, for about 5 minutes without browning.

3 Add the potatoes, vegetable bouillon, lemon juice, nutmeg, coriander, and bay leaf to the pan. Season to taste with salt and pepper and bring to a boil. Cover and simmer for 30 minutes, until all the vegetables are very soft.

4 Cool the soup a little. Remove and discard the bay leaf and then press through a strainer or process in a food processor or blender until smooth. Pour into a clean pan.

5 Blend the egg yolk into the cream. Add a little of the soup to this mixture and then whisk it all back into the soup. Reheat the soup gently, without boiling. Adjust the seasoning to taste if necessary. Cool, and then chill thoroughly in the refrigerator.

6 Serve the chilled soup garnished with a sprinkling of freshly snipped chives.

NUTRITION
Calories 208; Sugars 5 g; Protein 5 g;
Carbohydrate 20 g; Fat 12 g; Saturates 6 g

very easy

10 mins

40 mins

This is a really filling soup, which should be served before a light entrée. It is easy to prepare and filled with flavor.

Vegetable *and* Corn Chowder

1 Heat the oil in a large pan. Add the onion, bell pepper, garlic, and potato and sauté over low heat, stirring frequently, for 2–3 minutes.

2 Stir in the flour and cook, stirring for 30 seconds. Gradually stir in the milk and bouillon.

3 Add the broccoli and corn kernels. Bring the mixture to a boil, stirring constantly, then reduce the heat and simmer for about 20 minutes, or until all the vegetables are tender.

4 Add ½ cup of the cheese and stir until it melts.

5 Season and spoon the chowder into a warm soup tureen. Garnish with the remaining cheese and the chopped cilantro and serve.

SERVES 4

1 tbsp vegetable oil
1 red onion, diced
1 red bell pepper, halved, seeded, and diced
3 garlic cloves, crushed
1¾ cups diced potatoes
2 tbsp all-purpose flour
2½ cups milk
1¼ cups Fresh Vegetable Bouillon (see page 16)
½ cup broccoli flowerets
3 cups canned corn kernels, drained
¾ cup grated vegetarian colby cheese
salt and pepper
1 tbsp chopped fresh cilantro, to garnish

NUTRITION
Calories *378*; Sugars *20 g*; Protein *16 g*;
Carbohydrate *52 g*; Fat *13 g*; Saturates *6 g*

⊛⊛⊛   moderate
🖐   15 mins
🕐   20 mins

🍳 **COOK'S TIP**

Vegetarian cheeses are made with rennets of non-animal origin, using microbial or fungal enzymes.

Dhal is a delicious Indian lentil dish. This soup is a variation on the theme, made with red lentils and spiced with curry powder.

Curried Lentil Soup

SERVES 4

2 tbsp butter
2 garlic cloves, finely chopped
1 onion, chopped
½ tsp turmeric
1 tsp garam masala
¼ tsp chili powder
1 tsp ground cumin
2 lb/900 g canned, chopped tomatoes, drained
1 cup red lentils, washed
2 tsp lemon juice
2½ cups Fresh Vegetable Bouillon (see page 16)
1¼ cups coconut milk
salt and pepper
chopped fresh cilantro and lemon slices, to garnish
nan bread, to serve

1 Melt the butter in a large pan and sauté the garlic and onion for 2–3 minutes, stirring. Add the spices and cook for a further 30 seconds.

2 Stir in the tomatoes, red lentils, lemon juice, vegetable bouillon, and coconut milk, and bring to a boil.

3 Reduce the heat and simmer for 25–30 minutes until the lentils are tender and cooked.

4 Season to taste and spoon the soup into a warm tureen. Garnish and serve with warm nan bread.

NUTRITION
Calories *284*; Sugars *13 g*; Protein *16 g*; Carbohydrate *38 g*; Fat *9 g*; Saturates *5 g*

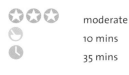

moderate

10 mins

35 mins

🎩 **COOK'S TIP**

You can buy cans of coconut milk from stores and delicatessens. It can also be made by grating creamed coconut, which comes in the form of a solid bar, and mixing it with water.

Beans feature widely in Mexican cooking, and here pinto beans are used to give an interesting texture. Pinto beans require soaking overnight.

Bean Soup

1 Drain the beans, rinse and place in a pan with the water. Bring to a boil and boil vigorously for 10 minutes. Lower the heat, cover, and simmer for 2 hours, or until the beans are tender.

2 Add the carrots, onion, garlic, chile, and bouillon and bring back to a boil. Cover and simmer for a further 30 minutes, until very tender.

3 Remove half the beans and vegetables with the cooking juices and press through a strainer or process in a food processor or blender until smooth.

4 Return the bean purée to the pan and add the tomatoes and celery. Simmer for 10–15 minutes, or until the celery is just tender, adding a little more bouillon or water if necessary.

5 Meanwhile, prepare the croûtons. Dice the bread. Heat the oil with the garlic in a small skillet and cook the croûtons until golden brown. Drain on paper towels.

6 Season the soup and stir in the chopped cilantro, if using. Transfer to a warm tureen and serve immediately with the croûtons.

COOK'S TIP

Pinto beans are widely available, but if you cannot find them or you wish to vary the recipe, you can use cannellini beans or black-eyed peas as an alternative.

SERVES 4

1 cup pinto beans, soaked overnight in water
5 cups water
1½ –2 cups carrots, finely chopped
1 large onion, finely chopped
2–3 garlic cloves, crushed
½ –1 chile, seeded and finely chopped
4 cups Fresh Vegetable Bouillon
   (see page 16)
2 tomatoes, peeled and finely chopped
2 celery stalks, very thinly sliced
salt and pepper
1 tbsp chopped fresh cilantro (optional)

croutons
3 slices white bread, crusts removed
oil, for deep-frying
1–2 garlic cloves, crushed

NUTRITION
Calories *188*; Sugars *9 g*; Protein *13 g*;
Carbohydrate *33 g*; Fat *1 g*; Saturates *0.3 g*

easy
8 hrs 20 mins
3 hrs

A thick and hearty soup, nourishing and substantial enough to serve as an entrée with warmed whole-wheat bread.

Indian Bean Soup

SERVES 4

4 tbsp vegetable ghee or vegetable oil
2 onions, peeled and chopped
½ lb/225 g potatoes, cut into chunks
½ lb/225 g parsnips, cut into chunks
½ lb/225 g turnips or rutabaga,
 cut into chunks
2 celery stalks, sliced
2 zucchini, sliced
1 green bell pepper, halved, deseeded
 and cut into ½-inch/1-cm pieces
2 garlic cloves, crushed
2 tsp ground coriander
1 tbsp paprika
1 tbsp mild curry paste
5 cups Fresh Vegetable Bouillon
 (see page 16)
salt
1½ cups canned black-eyed peas, drained
 and rinsed
chopped fresh cilantro, to garnish (optional)

NUTRITION
Calories *237*; Sugars *9 g*; Protein *9 g*;
Carbohydrate *33 g*; Fat *9 g*; Saturates *1 g*

⭐ very easy

🕐 15 mins

🕐 50 mins

1 Heat the ghee or oil in a pan, add all the prepared vegetables, except the zucchini and green bell pepper, and cook over moderate heat, stirring frequently, for 5 minutes. Add the garlic, ground coriander, paprika, and curry paste and cook, stirring constantly, for 1 minute.

2 Stir in the bouillon and season with salt to taste. Bring to a boil, cover, and simmer over a low heat, stirring occasionally, for 25 minutes.

3 Stir in the black-eyed peas, sliced zucchini, and green bell pepper, then replace the lid and continue cooking for a further 15 minutes, or until all the vegetables are tender.

4 Process 1¼ cups of the soup mixture (about 2 ladlefuls) in a food processor or blender. Return the puréed mixture to the soup in the pan and reheat until piping hot. Sprinkle with chopped cilantro if using, and serve hot.

Make the most of home-grown herbs to create this wonderfully creamy soup with its marvelous fresh aroma.

Cream Cheese *and* Herb Soup

1 Melt the butter or margarine in a large, heavy pan. Add the onions and cook over medium heat for 2 minutes, then cover and turn the heat to low. Continue to cook the onions for 5 minutes, then remove the lid.

2 Add the vegetable bouillon and herbs to the pan. Bring to a boil over moderate heat. Lower the heat, cover, and simmer gently for 20 minutes.

3 Remove the pan from the heat. Transfer the soup to a food processor or blender and process for about 15 seconds, until smooth. Alternatively, press it through a strainer with the back of a wooden spoon. Place the soup back in the pan.

4 Reserve a little of the cheese for garnish. Spoon the remaining cheese into the soup and whisk until it has melted and is incorporated.

5 Mix the cornstarch with the milk to a paste, then stir the mixture into the soup. Heat, stirring constantly, until thickened and smooth.

6 Pour the soup into warmed individual bowls. Spoon some of the reserved cheese into each bowl and garnish with chives. Serve at once.

SERVES 4

2 tbsp butter or margarine
2 onions, chopped
3½ cups Fresh Vegetable Bouillon (see page 16)
3 tbsp coarsely chopped mixed fresh herbs, such as parsley, chives, thyme, basil, and oregano
1 cup full-fat soft cheese
1 tbsp cornstarch
1 tbsp milk
chopped fresh chives, to garnish

NUTRITION
Calories 275; Sugars 5 g; Protein 0 g; Carbohydrate 14 g; Fat 22 g; Saturates 11 g

⭐ very easy

◔ 15 mins

🕐 35 mins

Appetizers

With so many fresh ingredients readily available, it is very easy to create some deliciously different appetizers to make the perfect introduction to a vegetarian meal. The ideas in this chapter are an inspiration to cook and a treat to eat, and they give an edge to the appetite that makes the main course even more enjoyable. When choosing an appetizer, make sure that you provide a good balance of flavors, colors, and textures that offer variety and contrast. Balance the nature of the recipes too—a rich main course is best preceded by a light appetizer, which is just enough to interest the palate and stimulate the taste buds.

Anyone who loves garlic will adore this dip—it is very potent! Serve it at a barbecue and dip raw vegetables or chunks of French bread into it.

Heavenly Garlic Dip

SERVES 4

2 garlic bulbs
6 tbsp olive oil
1 small onion, finely chopped
2 tbsp lemon juice
3 tbsp tahini sesame seed paste
2 tbsp chopped fresh parsley
salt and pepper

to serve
fresh vegetable crudités
French sticks, sliced, or warmed pitas

1 Separate the garlic bulbs into individual cloves. Place them on a cookie sheet and roast in a preheated oven, 400°F/200°C, for 8–10 minutes. Set them aside to cool for a few minutes. When they are cool enough to handle, peel the garlic cloves and then finely chop them.

3 Heat the olive oil in a pan or skillet and add the garlic and onion. Sauté over low heat, stirring occasionally, for 8–10 minutes, until soft. Remove the pan from the heat.

4 Mix in the lemon juice, tahini, and parsley. Season to taste with salt and pepper. Transfer the dip to a small heatproof bowl and keep warm at one side of the barbecue grill.

5 Serve with fresh vegetable crudités, or with chunks of French bread or warm pocket breads.

NUTRITION
Calories *344*; Sugars *2 g*; Protein *6 g*;
Carbohydrate *3 g*; Fat *34 g*; Saturates *5 g*

⭐ very easy
🕐 15 mins
🕐 20 mins

👨‍🍳 **COOK'S TIP**

If you come across smoked garlic, use it in this recipe—it tastes wonderful. There is no need to roast the smoked garlic, so omit the first step. This dip can also be used to baste vegetarian burgers.

This tasty dip is very easy to make. It is perfect to have at barbecues, as it gives your guests something to nibble on while they are waiting.

Buttered Nut *and* Lentil Dip

1 Melt half the butter in a pan, add the onion and sauté over medium heat, stirring frequently, until it is golden brown in color.

2 Add the lentils and vegetable bouillon. Bring to a boil, then reduce the heat and simmer gently, uncovered, for about 25–30 minutes, until the lentils are tender. Drain well.

3 Melt the remaining butter in a small skillet. Add the almonds and pine nuts and cook them over low heat, stirring frequently, until golden brown. Remove the pan from the heat.

4 Put the lentils, the almonds, and the pine nuts into a food processor or blender, together with any butter remaining in the skillet. Add the ground coriander, cumin, ginger, and fresh cilantro. Process for about 15–20 seconds, until the mixture is smooth. Alternatively, press the lentils through a strainer with the back of a wooden spoon to purée them and then mix with the finely chopped nuts, spices, and herbs.

5 Season the dip with salt and pepper and garnish with fresh cilantro sprigs. Serve with fresh vegetable crudités and bread sticks.

COOK'S TIP

Green or brown lentils can be used, but they will take longer to cook than red lentils. If you wish, substitute peanuts for the almonds. Ground ginger can be used instead of fresh—substitute ½ teaspoon and add it with the other spices.

SERVES 4

4 tbsp butter
1 small onion, chopped
½ cup red lentils, washed
1¼ cups Fresh Vegetable Bouillon (see page 16)
¾ cups blanched almonds
½ cup pine nuts
½ tsp ground coriander
½ tsp ground cumin
½ tsp grated fresh gingerroot
1 tsp chopped fresh cilantro
salt and pepper
fresh coriander sprigs to garnish

to serve
fresh vegetable crudités
bread sticks

NUTRITION
Calories *395*; Sugars *4 g*; Protein *12 g*; Carbohydrate *18 g*; Fat *31 g*; Saturates *10 g*

easy
5–10 mins
40 mins

This wonderful soft cheese pâté is fragrant with the aroma of fresh herbs and garlic. Serve with triangles of Melba toast for a perfect appetizer.

Cheese, Garlic *and* Herb Pâté

SERVES 4

1 tbsp butter
1 garlic clove, crushed
3 scallions, finely chopped
½ cup full-fat soft cheese
2 tbsp chopped mixed fresh herbs, such as parsley, chives, marjoram, oregano, and basil
1½ cups finely grated sharp Colby cheese
salt and pepper
4–6 slices of white bread from a medium-cut sliced loaf

to serve
mixed salad greens
cherry tomatoes

to garnish
ground paprika
fresh herb sprigs

1 Melt the butter in a small skillet and gently sauté the garlic and scallions together for 3–4 minutes, until soft. Let them cool.

2 Beat the soft cheese in a large mixing bowl until smooth, then add the garlic and scallions. Stir in the chopped mixed fresh herbs, mixing well.

3 Add the cheese and work the mixture together, seasoning to taste, to form a stiff paste. Cover and chill until ready to serve.

4 To make the Melba toast, toast the slices of bread on both sides, and then cut off the crusts. Using a sharp bread knife, cut through the slices horizontally to make very thin slices. Cut into triangles and then lightly toast the untoasted sides until golden.

5 Arrange the mixed salad greens on 4 serving plates with the cherry tomatoes. Pile the cheese pâté on top and sprinkle with a little paprika. Garnish with fresh herbs sprigsand serve with the Melba toast.

NUTRITION
Calories *392*; Sugars *1 g*; Protein *17 g*;
Carbohydrate *18 g*; Fat *28 g*; Saturates *18 g*

⭐ very easy

🕑 20 mins

🕐 10 mins

Red lentils are used in this spicy recipe for speed as they do not require presoaking. If you use other lentils, soak and precook them first.

Lentil Pâté

1 Heat the vegetable oil in a large pan and sauté the onion and garlic for 2–3 minutes, stirring. Add the spices and cook for a further 30 seconds. Stir in the vegetable bouillon and lentils and bring the mixture to a boil. Reduce the heat and simmer for 20 minutes or until the lentils are soft. Remove the pan from the heat and drain off any excess moisture.

2 Put the mixture in a food processor and add the egg, milk, mango chutney, and parsley. Blend until smooth.

3 Grease and line the base of a 1 lb loaf pan and spoon the mixture into the pan. Cover and cook in a preheated oven, 400°F/200°C, for 40–45 minutes or until firm.

4 Let the pâté cool in the pan for 20 minutes, then transfer to the refrigerator to cool completely. Slice the pâté and garnish with chopped fresh parsley. Serve with salad greens and warm toast.

SERVES 4

1 tbsp vegetable oil, plus extra for greasing
1 onion, chopped
2 garlic cloves, crushed
1 tsp garam masala
½ tsp ground coriander
3½ cups Fresh Vegetable Bouillon (see page 16)
1 cup red lentils, washed
1 small egg
2 tbsp milk
2 tbsp mango chutney
2 tbsp chopped fresh parsley, plus extra to garnish

to serve
salad greens
warm toast

NUTRITION
Calories *267*; Sugars *12 g*; Protein *14 g*; Carbohydrate *37 g*; Fat *8 g*; Saturates *1 g*

⭐⭐ easy
🥄 40 mins
🕐 1 hr 15 mins

🍳 **COOK'S TIP**

Use other spices, such as chili powder or Chinese five-spice powder, to flavor the pâté, and add tomato relish or chile relish instead of the mango chutney, if you prefer.

This is a really quick appetizer to prepare if canned beans are used. Choose a wide variety of beans for color and flavor.

Mixed Bean Pâté

SERVES 4

1½–2 cups canned mixed beans, drained
2 tbsp olive oil
juice of 1 lemon
2 garlic cloves, crushed
1 tbsp chopped fresh cilantro
2 scallions, chopped
salt and pepper
shredded scallions, to garnish

1 Rinse the beans thoroughly under cold running water and drain well.

2 Transfer the beans to a food processor or blender and process until smooth. Alternatively, place the beans in a bowl and mash thoroughly by hand with a fork or potato masher.

3 Add the olive oil, lemon juice, garlic, cilantro, and scallions and blend until fairly smooth. Season with salt and pepper to taste.

4 Transfer the pâté to a serving bowl, cover, and chill in the refrigerator for at least 30 minutes.

5 Garnish the pâté with shredded scallions and serve.

NUTRITION
Calories *126*; Sugars *3 g*; Protein *5 g*;
Carbohydrate *13 g*; Fat *6 g*; Saturates *1 g*

very easy

45 mins

0 mins

If you use frozen spinach, it only needs to be thawed and drained before being mixed with the cheeses and seasonings.

Spinach Filo Baskets

1 If using fresh spinach, cook it in the minimum of boiling salted water for 3–4 minutes, until tender. Drain very thoroughly, using a potato masher to remove excess liquid, then chop and put into a bowl. If using frozen spinach, simply thaw, drain, and chop.

2 Add the scallions or onion, garlic, cheeses, allspice, egg yolk, and seasoning, and mix well.

3 Grease 2 individual muffin pans, or alternatively use ovenproof dishes or pans about 5 inches/12 cm in diameter, and 1½ inches/4 cm deep. Cut the phyllo pastry sheets in half to make 8 pieces and brush each piece lightly with the melted butter.

4 Place 1 piece of phyllo pastry in a pan or dish and then cover with a second piece at right angles to the first. Add two more pieces at angles, so that all the corners are in different places. Line the other pan in the same way.

5 Spoon the spinach mixture into the "baskets" and cook in a preheated oven, 350°F/180°C, for about 20 minutes, or until the pastry is golden brown. Garnish each basket with a scallion tassel (see Cook's Tip) and serve them hot or cold.

✺ COOK'S TIP

Make the scallion tassels about 30 minutes before required. Trim off the root end and cut to a length of 2–3 inches/5–7 cm. Make a series of cuts from the green end to within ¾ inch/2 cm of the other end. Place in a bowl of iced water to open out. Drain well before use.

SERVES 4

3 cups fresh leaf spinach, washed and roughly chopped, or ½ cup thawed frozen spinach
2–4 scallions, trimmed and chopped, or 1 tbsp finely chopped onion
1 garlic clove, crushed
2 tbsp grated Parmesan cheese
¾ cup grated sharp colby cheese
pinch of ground allspice
1 egg yolk
4 sheets phyllo pastry
2 tbsp butter, melted
salt and pepper
2 scallions, to garnish

NUTRITION
Calories 533; Sugars 3 g; Protein 24 g; Carbohydrate 26 g; Fat 38 g; Saturates 22 g

⭐⭐⭐ moderate
🕐 30 mins
🕐 25 mins

These crisp-baked bread cases, filled with sliced tomatoes, feta cheese, black olives, and quail's eggs, are quick to make and taste delicious.

Feta Cheese Tartlets

SERVES 4

8 slices bread from a medium-cut large loaf
½ cup, plus 1 tbsp butter, melted
1 cup feta cheese, cut into small cubes
4 cherry tomatoes, cut into wedges
8 pitted black or green olives, halved
8 quail's eggs, hard-cooked
2 tbsp olive oil
1 tbsp wine vinegar
1 tsp whole-grain mustard
pinch of superfine sugar
salt and pepper
fresh parsley sprigs, to garnish

1 Remove the crusts from the bread. Trim the bread into squares and flatten each piece with a rolling pin.

2 Brush the bread squares with melted butter, and then arrange them in bun or muffin pans. Press a piece of crumpled foil into each bread case to secure in place. Bake the cases in a preheated oven, 375°F/190°C, for about 10 minutes, or until crisp and browned.

3 Meanwhile, mix together the feta cheese, tomatoes, and olives. Shell the eggs and quarter them. Mix together the olive oil, vinegar, mustard, and sugar. Season to taste with salt and pepper.

4 Remove the bread cases from the oven and discard the foil. Let cool.

5 Just before serving, fill the bread cases with the cheese and tomato mixture. Arrange the eggs on top and spoon over the dressing. Garnish with fresh parsley sprigs.

NUTRITION
Calories 570; Sugars 3 g; Protein 14 g;
Carbohydrate 36 g; Fat 42 g; Saturates 23 g

⭐ very easy

🕑 30 mins

🕐 10 mins

Hummus is a real favorite spread on these garlic toasts for a delicious appetizer or as part of a nutritious light lunch.

Hummus Toasts *with* Olives

1 To make the hummus, firstly drain the garbanzo beans, reserving the liquid. Put the garbanzo beans and a little of the liquid in a food processor and blend, gradually adding more reserved liquid and the lemon juice. Blend well after each addition until smooth.

2 Stir in the sesame seed paste and all but 1 teaspoon of the olive oil. Add the garlic, season to taste, and blend again until smooth.

3 Spoon the hummus into a serving dish. Drizzle the remaining olive oil over the top, and garnish with chopped cilantro and olives. Let chill in the refrigerator while preparing the toasts.

4 Lay the slices of ciabatta on a broiler rack in a single layer.

5 Mix the garlic, cilantro, and olive oil together and drizzle over the bread slices. Cook under a hot broiler for 2–3 minutes, until golden brown, turning once. Serve hot with the hummus.

SERVES 4

1½ cups canned garbanzo beans
juice of 1 large lemon
6 tbsp tahini sesame seed paste
2 tbsp olive oil
2 garlic cloves, finely chopped
salt and pepper
1 ciabatta loaf, sliced
2 garlic cloves, finely chopped
1 tbsp chopped fresh cilantro
4 tbsp olive oil

to garnish
chopped fresh cilantro
black olives

NUTRITION
Calories *731*; Sugars *2 g*; Protein *22 g*;
Carbohydrate *39 g*; Fat *55 g*; Saturates *8 g*

✪✪✪   moderate

🕐   15 mins

🕐   2–3 mins

This is a well-known method of cooking vegetables and is perfect with shallots or onions, served with a crisp salad.

Onions *à la* Grecque

SERVES 4

1 lb/450 g shallots
3 tbsp olive oil
3 tbsp clear honey
2 tbsp garlic wine vinegar
3 tbsp dry white wine
1 tbsp tomato paste
2 celery stalks, sliced
2 tomatoes, seeded and chopped
salt and pepper
chopped celery leaves, to garnish

1 Peel the shallots. Heat the oil in a large pan, add the shallots and cook, stirring, for 3–5 minutes, or until they begin to brown.

2 Add the honey and cook over a high heat for a further 30 seconds, then add the garlic wine vinegar and dry white wine, stirring well.

3 Stir in the tomato paste, the celery, and the tomatoes, and bring the mixture to a boil. Cook over a high heat for 5–6 minutes. Season to taste with salt and pepper and let cool slightly.

4 Garnish with chopped celery leaves and serve warm. Alternatively chill in the refrigerator before serving.

NUTRITION
Calories *200*; Sugars *26 g*; Protein *2 g*;
Carbohydrate *28 g*; Fat *9 g*; Saturates *1 g*

⭐ very easy

🕐 10 mins

🕐 15 mins

Make this Mexican-style salsa to perk up jaded palates. Its lively flavors really get the taste buds going. Serve with hot tortilla chips.

Fiery Salsa

1 Remove and discard the stem and seeds from 1 fresh red chile. Chop the flesh very finely and place in a large mixing bowl.

2 Use the other red chile to make a "flower" for the garnish. Using a small, sharp knife, slice the remaining chile from the stem to the tip several times without removing the stem, so the slices remain attached. Place in a bowl of ice water so that the "petals" open out.

3 Add the lime juice to the chile in the mixing bowl. Halve, pit, and peel the avocados. Add the flesh to the mixing bowl and mash thoroughly with a fork. The salsa should be slightly chunky. (The lime juice prevents the avocado from turning brown.)

4 Finely chop the cucumber and tomatoes and add to the avocado mixture with the crushed garlic.

5 Stir in the Tabasco sauce and season with salt and pepper. Transfer the salsa to a serving bowl. Garnish with slices of lime and the chile flower.

6 Put the bowl on a large plate, surround with tortilla chips, and serve. Do not keep this dip standing for long or it will discolor.

SERVES 4

2 small fresh red chiles
1 tbsp lime or lemon juice
2 large ripe avocados
2-inch/5-cm piece of cucumber
2 tomatoes, peeled
1 small garlic clove, crushed
dash of Tabasco sauce
salt and pepper
lime or lemon slices, to garnish
tortilla chips, to serve

NUTRITION
Calories 328; Sugars 2 g; Protein 4 g;
Carbohydrate 21 g; Fat 26 g; Saturates 5 g

⭐⭐   easy
🕐   30 mins
🕐   0 mins

Thin slices of vegetables are wrapped in pastry and deep-fried until crisp. Spring roll wrappers are available fresh or frozen.

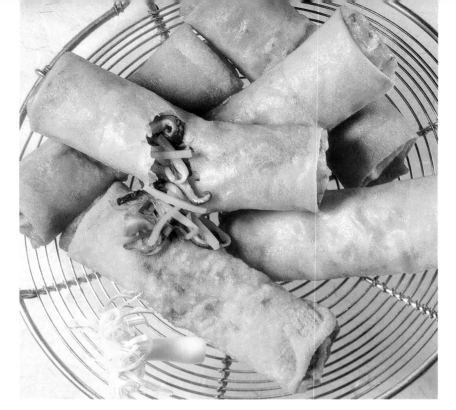

Spring Rolls

MAKES 12

5 Chinese dried mushrooms
    (if unavailable, use open-cup mushrooms)
2 tbsp vegetable oil
1 large carrot, cut into matchsticks
1 cup canned bamboo shoots,
    cut into matchsticks
2 scallions
2 oz/55 g Chinese cabbage, shredded
4 cups beansprouts
1 tbsp soy sauce
12 spring roll wrappers
1 egg, beaten
vegetable oil, for deep-frying
salt

1 Place the dried mushrooms in a small bowl and cover with warm water. Leave to soak for 20–25 minutes.

2 Drain the mushrooms and squeeze out the excess water. Remove the tough centers and slice the mushroom caps thinly.

3 Heat the 2 tablespoons of oil in a wok. Add the mushrooms, carrot, and bamboo shoots and stir-fry for 2 minutes. Add the scallions, Chinese cabbage, beansprouts, and soy sauce. Season with salt and stir-fry for 2 minutes. Leave to cool.

4 Divide the mixture into 12 equal portions and place one portion on the edge of each spring roll wrapper. Fold in the sides and roll each one up, brushing the join with a little beaten egg to seal.

5 Deep-fry the spring rolls in batches in hot oil in a wok or large pan for 4–5 minutes, or until golden and crispy. Take care that the oil is not too hot or the spring rolls will brown on the outside before cooking on the inside. Remove and drain on paper towels. Keep each batch warm while the others are being cooked. Serve at once.

NUTRITION
Calories *186*; Sugars *2 g*; Protein *4 g*;
Carbohydrate *18 g*; Fat *11 g*; Saturates *1 g*

easy

45 mins

25–30 mins

Crispy coated vegetables and bean curd, with a sweet, spicy dip, give a real taste of Asia in this Japanese-style dish.

Bean Curd Tempura

1 Slice the zucchini and carrots in half lengthwise. Trim the corn. Trim the leeks at both ends. Cut the eggplants into fourth lengthwise. Cut the bean curd into 1-inch/2.5-cm cubes.

2 To make the batter, mix the egg yolks with the water. Sift in 1¼ cups of the flour and beat with a balloon whisk to form a thick batter. Don't worry if there are any lumps. Heat the oil for deep-frying to 350°F/180°C, or until a cube of bread browns in 30 seconds.

3 Place the remaining flour on a large plate and toss the vegetables and bean curd until lightly coated.

4 Dip the bean curd in the batter and deep-fry for 2–3 minutes, until lightly golden. Drain on paper towels and keep warm.

5 Dip the vegetables in the batter and deep-fry, a few at a time, for 3–4 minutes, until golden. Drain and place on a warmed serving plate.

6 To make the dipping sauce, mix all the ingredients together. Serve with the vegetables and bean curd, accompanied with noodles and garnished with julienne strips of vegetables.

SERVES 4

¼ lb/115 g baby zucchini
¼ lb/115 g baby carrots
¼ lb/115 g baby corn ears
¼ lb/115 g baby leeks
2 baby eggplants
8 oz/225 g bean curd
vegetable oil, for deep-frying
julienne strips of carrot, gingerroot, and
    baby leek, to garnish
noodles, to serve

batter
2 egg yolks
1¼ cups water
1½ cups all-purpose flour

dipping sauce
5 tbsp mirin or dry sherry
5 tbsp Japanese soy sauce
2 tsp clear honey
1 garlic clove, crushed
1 tsp grated fresh gingerroot

NUTRITION
Calories 582; Sugars 10 g; Protein 16 g;
Carbohydrate 65 g; Fat 27 g; Saturates 4 g

⭐ very easy

🕑 15 mins

🕐 20 mins

These small bhajis are often served as an accompaniment but are also delicious served as an appetizer with a small salad and yogurt sauce.

Mixed Bhajis

SERVES 4

bhajis
1 cup gram (besan) flour
1 tsp baking soda
2 tsp ground coriander
1 tsp garam masala
1½ tsp turmeric
1½ tsp chili powder
2 tbsp chopped fresh cilantro
1 small onion, halved and sliced
1 small leek, sliced
1 cup cooked cauliflower
9–12 tbsp cold water
salt and pepper
vegetable oil, for deep-frying

sauce
2/3 cup plain yogurt
2 tbsp chopped fresh mint
½ tsp ground turmeric
1 garlic clove, crushed
fresh mint sprigs, to garnish

NUTRITION
Calories *414*; Sugars *7 g*; Protein *9 g*;
Carbohydrate *38 g*; Fat *26 g*; Saturates *3 g*

⭐⭐ easy
🕐 25 mins
🕐 20 mins

1 Strain the flour, baking soda, and salt to taste into a mixing bowl and add the spices and fresh cilantro. Mix together thoroughly.

2 Divide the mixture into three and place in separate bowls. Stir the onion into one bowl, the leek into another, and the cauliflower into the third bowl. Add 3–4 tablespoons of water to each bowl and mix each to form a smooth paste.

3 Heat the vegetable oil in a deep fryer to 350°F/180°C or until a cube of bread browns in 30 seconds. Using 2 dessert spoons, form the mixture into rounds and cook each in the oil for 3–4 minutes, until browned.

4 Remove the bhajis with a slotted spoon, drain well on absorbent paper towels, and keep warm in the oven while cooking the remainder.

5 Mix the sauce ingredients together, garnish with mint sprigs, and serve with the warm bhajis.

This is a very versatile dish that will go with almost anything and can be served warm or cold. It is perfect as an appetizer for a dinner party.

Hyderabad Pickles

1 Dry-roast the coriander, cumin, coconut, sesame seeds, and mustard and onion seeds in a skillet until lightly colored and the spices release their aroma. Grind in a pestle and mortar or food processor and set aside.

2 Heat the oil in a skillet and sauté the onions until golden. Reduce the heat and add the ginger, garlic, turmeric, chili powder, and salt, stirring. Let cool, then grind this mixture to form a paste.

3 Make 4 cuts across each eggplant half. Blend the spices with the onion paste. Spoon this mixture into the slits in the eggplants.

4 In a bowl, mix the tamarind paste and 3 tablespoons of the water to make a fine paste and set aside.

5 For the baghaar, sauté the onion and mustard seeds, cumin seeds, and dried red chilies in the oil. Reduce the heat, place the eggplants in the baghaar, and stir gently. Stir in the tamarind paste and 1 cup of water and cook over a medium heat for 15–20 minutes. Add the cilantro and the chopped green chile.

6 When cool, transfer to a serving dish and serve garnished with the hard-cooked eggs.

SERVES 4

2 tsp coriander seeds
2 tsp cumin seeds
2 tsp shredded coconut
2 tsp sesame seeds
1 tsp mixed mustard and onion seeds
1¼ cups vegetable oil
3 medium onions, sliced
1 tsp finely chopped fresh gingerroot
1 tsp crushed garlic
½ tsp turmeric
1½ tsp chili powder
1½ tsp salt
3 medium eggplants, halved lengthwise
1 tbsp tamarind paste
3 hard-cooked eggs, halved, to garnish

baghaar
1 tsp mixed onion and mustard seeds
1 tsp cumin seeds
4 dried red chilis
⅔ cup vegetable oil
cilantro leaves, and 1 fresh green chile, chopped finely

NUTRITION

Calories *732*; Sugars *6 g*; Protein *6 g*; Carbohydrate *8 g*; Fat *75 g*; Saturates *10 g*

✪✪ easy

30 mins

30 mins

Whole mushrooms are dunked in a spiced garlicky batter and deep-fried until golden. They are at their most delicious served piping hot.

Garlicky Mushroom Pakoras

SERVES 4

1 cup gram (besan) flour
½ tsp salt
¼ tsp baking powder
1 tsp cumin seeds
½–1 tsp chili powder
¾ cup water
2 garlic cloves, crushed
1 small onion, finely chopped
vegetable oil, for deep-frying
1 lb/450 g white mushrooms, trimmed and wiped

to garnish
lemon wedges
cilantro sprigs

1 Put the gram flour, salt, baking powder, cumin, and chili powder into a bowl and mix well together. Make a well in the center of the mixture and gradually stir in the water, mixing thoroughly to form a batter.

2 Stir the garlic and onion into the batter and let the mixture infuse for 10 minutes. One-third fill a deep fryer or pan with vegetable oil and heat to 350°F/180°C or until a cube of bread browns in 30 seconds. Lower the basket into the hot oil.

3 Meanwhile, mix the mushrooms into the batter, stirring to coat. Remove a few at a time and place them into the hot oil. Sauté for about 2 minutes, or until golden brown.

4 Remove the mushrooms from the pan with a draining spoon and drain on paper towels while you are cooking the remainder in the same way.

5 Serve hot, sprinkled with coarse salt and garnished with lemon wedges and cilantro sprigs.

NUTRITION
Calories *297*; Sugars *3 g*; Protein *5 g*; Carbohydrate *24 g*; Fat *21 g*; Saturates *2 g*

easy

20 mins

10–15 mins

🍳 **COOK'S TIP**

Gram flour, also known as besan flour, is a pale yellow flour made from garbanzo beans. It is now readily available from larger food stores, as well as Indian food stores and some ethnic delicatessens.

Samosas, which are a sort of Indian pasty, make excellent snacks. In India, they are popular snacks at roadside stands.

Samosas

1 Strain the flour and salt into a bowl. Add the pieces of butter and rub into the flour until the mixture resembles fine bread crumbs.

2 Pour in the water and mix with a fork to form a dough. Pat it into a ball and knead for 5 minutes, or until smooth. Cover and let rise.

3 To make the filling, mash the boiled potatoes gently and mix with the ginger, garlic, white cumin seeds, onion and mustard seeds, salt, crushed red chiles, lemon juice, and green chiles.

4 Break small balls off the dough and roll each out very thinly to form a round. Cut in half, dampen the edges, and shape into cones. Fill the cones with a little of the filling, dampen the top and bottom edges of the cones, and pinch together to seal. Set aside.

5 Fill a deep pan one-third full with oil and heat to 350°F/180°C or until a small cube of bread browns in 30 seconds. Carefully lower the samosas into the oil, a few at a time, and cook for 2–3 minutes, or until golden brown. Remove from the oil and drain thoroughly on paper towels. Serve hot or cold.

MAKES 12

pastry
¾ cup self-rising flour
½ tsp salt
3 tbsp butter, cut into small pieces
4 tbsp water

filling
3 medium potatoes, boiled
1 tsp finely chopped fresh gingerroot
1 tsp crushed garlic
½ tsp white cumin seeds
½ tsp mixed onion and mustard seeds
1 tsp salt
½ tsp crushed fresh red chiles
2 tbsp lemon juice
2 small fresh green chiles, finely chopped
ghee or oil, for deep-frying

NUTRITION
Calories *261*; Sugars *0.4 g*; Protein *2 g*;
Carbohydrate *13 g*; Fat *23 g*; Saturates *4 g*

⭐⭐⭐   moderate
🕐   40 mins
🕐   15 mins

These are ideal with a more formal meal as they take little time to prepare and look really impressive.

Mini Vegetable Puff Pastries

SERVES 4

pastry

1 lb/450 g puff pie dough
1 egg, beaten

filling

½ lb/225 g sweet potatoes, cubed
12–16 baby asparagus spears
2 tbsp butter or margarine
1 leek, sliced
2 small open-cap mushrooms, sliced
1 tsp lime juice
1 tsp chopped fresh thyme
pinch of dried mustard
salt and pepper

1 Cut the pie dough into 4 equal pieces. Roll each piece out on a lightly floured counter to form a 5-inch/13-cm square. Place the pieces on a dampened cookie sheet and score a smaller 2½-inch/6-cm square inside.

2 Brush with beaten egg and cook in a preheated oven, 400°F/200°C, for 20 minutes or until risen and golden brown.

3 While the pie dough is cooking, start the filling. Cook the sweet potato in a pan of boiling water for 15 minutes, then drain well. Blanch the asparagus in a pan of boiling water for 10 minutes or until tender. Drain and reserve.

4 Remove the pastry squares from the oven. Cut out the central square of pastry and lift out. Reserve.

5 Melt the butter or margarine in a pan and sauté the sliced leek and mushrooms for 2–3 minutes. Add the lime juice, thyme, and mustard and season well. Stir in the sweet potatoes and asparagus. Spoon into the pastry cases. Top with the reserved pastry squares and serve immediately.

NUTRITION

Calories *210*; Sugars *2.3 g*; Protein *3.8 g*;
Carbohydrate *21 g*; Fat *13 g*; Saturates *1.7 g*

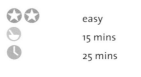

easy

15 mins

25 mins

COOK'S TIP

Use a colorful selection of any vegetables you have to hand for this recipe.

These individual soufflés make very impressive appetizers, but must be cooked just before serving to prevent them from sinking.

Mushroom *and* Garlic Soufflés

1 Lightly grease the inside of four ⅝ cup/150 ml individual soufflé dishes with a little butter.

2 Melt 2 tablespoons of the butter in a skillet. Add the mushrooms, lime juice, and garlic and sauté for 2–3 minutes, then remove the mushroom mixture with a slotted spoon and transfer it to a mixing bowl. Stir in the marjoram.

3 Melt the remaining butter in a pan. Add the flour and cook for 1 minute, then remove from the heat. Stir in the milk and return to the heat. Bring to a boil, stirring until thickened.

4 Mix the sauce into the mushroom mixture and beat in the egg yolks.

5 Whisk the egg whites until they form peaks and fold into the mushroom mixture until fully incorporated.

6 Divide the mixture between the prepared soufflé dishes. Place the dishes on a cookie sheet and cook in a preheated oven, 400°F/200°C, for about 8–10 minutes, or until the soufflés are well risen, golden brown, and cooked through. Serve immediately.

SERVES 4

4 tbsp butter
¾ cup finely chopped open-cap mushrooms
2 tsp lime juice
2 garlic cloves, crushed
2 tbsp chopped fresh marjoram
3½ tbsp all-purpose flour
1 cup milk
salt and pepper
2 eggs, separated

NUTRITION
Calories *179*; Sugars *3 g*; Protein *6 g*; Carbohydrate *8 g*; Fat *14 g*; Saturates *8 g*

⭐⭐ easy
🍳 10 mins
🕐 20 mins

COOK'S TIP

Insert a skewer into the center of the soufflés to test if they are cooked through—it should come out clean. If not, cook for a few minutes longer, but do not overcook otherwise they will become rubbery.

Light Meals

The ability to rustle up a simple snack or a quickly-prepared light meal can be very important in our busy lives. Sometimes we may not feel like eating a full-scale meal, but nevertheless want something appetizing and satisfying. Or if lunch or dinner is going to be served very late, then we may want something to tide us over and stave off those hunger pangs! Whether it is for a sustaining snack to break the day, or hearty nibbles to serve with predinner drinks, or an informal lunch or supper party, you'll find a mouthwatering collection of recipes in this chapter.

Roasted vegetables are delicious and attractive. Served on warm English muffins with a herb sauce, they are unbeatable.

Vegetable-Topped Muffins

SERVES 4

1 red onion, cut into 8 wedges
1 eggplant, halved and sliced
1 yellow bell pepper, halved, seeded, and sliced
1 zucchini, sliced
¼ cup olive oil
1 tbsp garlic vinegar
2 tbsp vermouth
2 garlic cloves, crushed
1 tbsp chopped fresh thyme
2 tsp light brown sugar
4 English muffins, halved

sauce
2 tbsp butter
1 tbsp all-purpose flour
⅔ cup milk
5 tbsp Fresh Vegetable Bouillon (see page 16)
¾ cup grated Colby cheese
1 tsp whole-grain mustard
3 tbsp chopped mixed fresh herbs
salt and pepper

NUTRITION
Calories 740; Sugars 27 g; Protein 20 g;
Carbohydrate 67 g; Fat 45 g; Saturates 17 g

★★★   moderate
🕐   1 hr 15 mins
🕐   35 mins

1 Arrange the onion, eggplant, yellow bell pepper, and zucchini in a shallow nonmetallic dish. Combine the olive oil, garlic vinegar, vermouth, garlic, thyme, and sugar and pour over the vegetables, turning to coat well. Let marinate for 1 hour.

2 Transfer the vegetables to a cookie sheet. Roast in a preheated oven, 400°F/200°C, for about 20–25 minutes or until the vegetables are softened.

3 Meanwhile, make the sauce. Melt the butter in a small pan and stir in the flour. Cook for 1 minute over low heat, stirring constantly, then remove the pan from the heat. Gradually stir in the milk and vegetable bouillon and return the pan to the heat. Bring to a boil, stirring constantly until thickened. Stir in the cheese, mustard, and mixed herbs and season well.

4 Cut the muffins in half and toast under a preheated broiler for 2–3 minutes until golden brown, then transfer to a serving plate. Spoon the roasted vegetables on top of the muffins and pour the sauce over. Serve immediately.

This warming Mexican dish consists of tortillas filled with a spicy vegetable mixture and topped with a hot tomato sauce.

Vegetable Enchiladas

1 To make the filling, blanch the spinach in a pan of boiling water for 2 minutes, drain well, and chop.

2 Heat the oil in a skillet and sauté the baby corn ears, peas, bell pepper, carrot, leek, garlic, and chile for 3–4 minutes, stirring briskly. Stir in the spinach and season well with salt and pepper, to taste.

3 Put all of the sauce ingredients in a pan and bring them to a boil, stirring constantly. Continue to cook over high heat for an additional 20 minutes, stirring, until the sauce has thickened and reduced by a third.

4 Spoon a quarter of the filling along the center of each tortilla. Roll the tortillas around the filling and place in an ovenproof dish, seam-side down.

5 Pour the tomato sauce over the tortillas and sprinkle the grated cheese on top. Cook in a preheated oven, 350°F/180°C, for 20 minutes or until the cheese is bubbling and golden. Serve the enchiladas immediately.

SERVES   4

4 tortillas
½ cup grated colby cheese

filling
1¼ tightly packed cups young spinach
2 tbsp olive oil
8 baby corn ears, sliced
¼ cup frozen peas, thawed
1 red bell pepper, halved, seeded, and diced
1 carrot, diced
1 leek, sliced
2 garlic cloves, crushed
1 fresh red chile, chopped
salt and pepper

sauce
1¼ cups strained tomatoes
2 shallots, chopped
1 garlic clove, crushed
1¼ cups Fresh Vegetable Bouillon
   (see page 16)
1 tsp superfine sugar
1 tsp chili powder

NUTRITION
Calories *309*; Sugars *14 g*; Protein *12 g*;
Carbohydrate *23 g*; Fat *19 g*; Saturates *8 g*

★★★   moderate

🕐   20 mins

🕐   50 mins

Crêpes are ideal for filling with your favorite ingredients. In this recipe they are packed with a deliciously spicy vegetable filling.

Vegetable Crêpes

SERVES 4

crepes
generous ³⁄₄ cup all-purpose flour
pinch of salt
1 egg, lightly beaten
1¹⁄₄ cups milk
vegetable oil, for frying

filling
2 tbsp vegetable oil
1 leek, shredded
¹⁄₂ tsp each chili powder and ground cumin
³⁄₄ cup snow peas
3¹⁄₂ oz/100 g white mushrooms,
1 red bell pepper, halved, seeded and sliced
4 tbsp cashew nuts, chopped

sauce
2 tbsp margarine
3 tbsp all-purpose flour
²⁄₃ cup Fresh Vegetable Bouillon
²⁄₃ cup milk
1 tsp Dijon mustard
³⁄₄ cup grated colby cheese
2 tbsp chopped fresh cilantro

NUTRITION
Calories *509*; Sugars *10 g*; Protein *17 g*;
Carbohydrate *36 g*; Fat *34 g*; Saturates *9 g*

moderate

15 mins

45 mins

1 For the crêpes, sift the flour and salt into a bowl. Beat in the egg and milk to make a batter.

2 For the filling, heat the oil and cook the leek for 2–3 minutes. Add the remaining ingredients and cook, stirring constantly, for 5 minutes.

3 For the sauce, melt the margarine and add the flour. Cook, stirring, for 1 minute. Remove from the heat, stir in the bouillon and milk, and return to the heat. Bring to a boil, stirring until thickened. Stir in the mustard, half the cheese, and the cilantro and cook for 1 minute.

4 To make the crêpes, heat 1 tablespoon of oil in a small skillet. Pour off the oil and add about 2¹⁄₂ tablespoons of the batter. Tilt to cover the base. Cook for 2 minutes, turn, and cook the other side for 1 minute. Remove the crêpe and keep warm. Repeat with the remaining batter. Spoon a little of the filling along the center of each crêpe and roll up. Place in a flameproof dish and pour the sauce on top. Top with cheese and heat under a hot broiler for 3–5 minutes or until the cheese melts.

This spicy rice dish is a vegetarian version of the traditional jambalaya. Packed with a variety of vegetables, it is both colorful and nutritious.

Vegetable Jambalaya

1 Cook the rice in a large pan of salted boiling water for 20 minutes, or until cooked through. Drain, rinse with boiling water, drain again, and set aside.

2 Heat the oil in a heavy skillet and cook the garlic and onion, stirring constantly, for 2–3 minutes. Add the eggplant, bell pepper, corn, peas, and broccoli flowerets to the skillet and cook, stirring occasionally, for a further 2–3 minutes.

3 Stir in the vegetable bouillon and the canned tomatoes, tomato paste, creole seasoning, and chili flakes.

4 Season to taste and cook over low heat for 15–20 minutes, or until the vegetables are tender.

5 Stir the brown rice into the vegetable mixture and cook, mixing well, for 3–4 minutes, or until hot.

6 Transfer the vegetable jambalaya to a warm serving dish and serve at once.

SERVES 4

½ cup brown rice (see Cook's Tip)
2 tbsp olive oil
2 garlic cloves, crushed
1 red onion, cut into 8 wedges
1 eggplant, diced
1 green bell pepper, halved, deseeded, and diced
5–6 baby corn ears, halved lengthwise
½ cup frozen peas
1 cup small broccoli flowerets
⅔ cup Fresh Vegetable Bouillon (see page 16)
1 cup chopped tomatoes
1 tbsp tomato paste
1 tsp creole seasoning
½ tsp chili flakes
salt and pepper

NUTRITION
Calories *181*; Sugars *8 g*; Protein *6 g*;
Carbohydrate *25 g*; Fat *7 g*; Saturates *1 g*

   easy
        10 mins
        50 mins

🍳 **COOK'S TIP**

Use a mixture of different kinds of rice, such as wild or red rice, to add color and texture to this dish. Cook the rice in advance, following the packet instructions, for a speedier recipe.

These spicy vegetable burgers are delicious, especially in a warm bun or roll and served with light French fries.

Vegetable Burgers *and* Fries

SERVES 4

vegetable burgers
4 oz/100 g spinach
2 tbsp olive oil
1 leek, chopped
2 garlic cloves, crushed
1⅓ cups chopped mushrooms
10½ oz/300 g firm bean curd, chopped
1 tsp chili powder
1 tsp curry powder
1 tbsp chopped fresh cilantro
1½ cups fresh whole-wheat bread crumbs

to serve
burger bap or roll
salad greens

french fries
2 large potatoes
2 tbsp all-purpose flour
1 tsp chili powder
2 tbsp olive oil

NUTRITION
Calories *461*; Sugars *4 g*; Protein *18 g*;
Carbohydrate *64 g*; Fat *17 g*; Saturates *2 g*

⭐⭐⭐   moderate
🕓   1hr 15 mins
🕓   1 hr

1 To make the burgers, cook the spinach in a little boiling water for 2 minutes. Drain thoroughly and pat dry with paper towels.

2 Heat 1 tablespoon of the oil in a skillet and sauté the leek and garlic for 2–3 minutes. Add the remaining ingredients, except the bread crumbs, and cook for 5–7 minutes until the vegetables are softened. Toss in the spinach and cook for 1 minute.

3 Transfer the mixture to a food processor and process for 30 seconds until almost smooth. Transfer to a bowl, stir in the bread crumbs, mixing well, and set aside until cool enough to handle. Using floured hands, form the mixture into 4 equal-size burgers. Chill for 30 minutes.

4 To make the fries, cut the potatoes into thin wedges and cook in a pan of boiling water for 10 minutes. Drain thoroughly and toss in the flour and chili powder. Lay the fries on a cookie sheet and sprinkle with the oil. Cook in a preheated oven, 400°F/200°C, for 30 minutes or until golden.

5 Meanwhile, heat the remaining oil in a skillet and cook the burgers for 8–10 minutes, turning once. Place in a bap, add some salad greens, and serve with the fries.

This is a very tasty, well-known Middle Eastern dish of small garbanzo bean balls, spiced and deep-fried.

Falafel

1 Put the garbanzo beans, onion, garlic, whole-wheat bread, chiles, spices, and cilantro in a food processor and process for 30 seconds. Stir the mixture and season to taste with salt and pepper.

2 Remove from the food processor and shape into walnut-sized balls.

3 Place the beaten egg in a shallow bowl and place the whole-wheat bread crumbs on a plate. First dip the garbanzo bean balls into the egg to coat them thoroughly and then roll them in the bread crumbs, shaking off any excess crumbs.

4 Heat the oil for deep-frying to 350°F/180°C, or until a cube of bread browns in 30 seconds. Cook the falafel, in batches if necessary, for 2–3 minutes, until crisp and browned. Carefully remove them from the oil with a slotted spoon and dry on absorbent paper towels.

5 Garnish the falafel with the reserved chopped cilantro and serve with a tomato and cucumber salad and lemon wedges.

SERVES 4

2³/₄ cups canned garbanzo beans, drained
1 red onion, chopped
3 garlic cloves, crushed
3–4 slices whole-wheat bread
2 small fresh red chiles
1 tsp ground cumin
1 tsp ground coriander
¹/₂ tsp turmeric
1 tbsp chopped cilantro, plus extra to garnish
1 egg, beaten
³/₄ cup whole-wheat bread crumbs
vegetable oil, for deep-frying
salt and pepper

to serve
tomato and cucumber salad
lemon wedges

NUTRITION
Calories *491*; Sugars *3 g*; Protein *15 g*;
Carbohydrate *43 g*; Fat *30 g*; Saturates *3 g*

easy

25 mins

10–15 mins

These are incredibly simple to make and sure to be popular served as a tempting snack or as an accompaniment to almost any Indian meal.

Potato Fritters *with* Relish

SERVES 4

¹⁄₃ cup all-purpose whole-wheat flour
¹⁄₂ tsp ground coriander
¹⁄₂ tsp cumin seeds
¹⁄₄ tsp chili powder
¹⁄₂ tsp ground turmeric
¹⁄₄ tsp salt
1 egg
3 tbsp milk
³⁄₄ lb/350 g potatoes, peeled
1–2 garlic cloves, crushed
4 scallions, chopped
¹⁄₄ cup corn kernels
vegetable oil, for shallow frying

onion & tomato relish

1 onion, peeled and diced
¹⁄₂ lb/225 g tomatoes, sliced
2 tbsp chopped fresh cilantro
2 tbsp chopped fresh mint
2 tbsp lemon juice
¹⁄₂ tsp roasted cumin seeds
¹⁄₄ tsp salt
pinch of cayenne pepper

NUTRITION

Calories *294*; Sugars *4 g*; Protein *4 g*;
Carbohydrate *18 g*; Fat *24 g*; Saturates *3 g*

⭐⭐   easy
🕐   40 mins
🕐   15 mins

1 First make the relish. Place all the ingredients for the relish in a bowl. Mix together well and let stand for at least 15 minutes before serving to let the flavors blend.

2 Place the flour in a bowl, stir in the spices and salt, and make a well in the center. Add the egg and milk and mix to form a fairly thick batter.

3 Coarsely grate the potatoes, place them in a strainer, and rinse well under cold running water. Drain and squeeze dry, then stir them into the batter with the garlic, scallions, and corn kernels, and mix to combine thoroughly.

4 Heat about ¹⁄₄-inch/5-mm of vegetable oil in a large skillet and add a few tablespoonfuls of the mixture at a time, flattening each one to form a thin fritter. Cook over low heat, turning frequently, for 2–3 minutes, or until golden brown and cooked through.

5 Drain the fritters on absorbent paper towels and keep them hot while cooking the remaining mixture in the same way. Serve the potato fritters hot with the onion and tomato relish.

These wafer-thin potato chips are great cooked over a barbecue grill and served with spicy vegetable kebabs.

Paprika Chips

1 Using a sharp knife, slice the potatoes very thinly so that they are almost transparent. Pat the potato slices dry with paper towels.

2 Heat the oil in a large skillet and add the paprika, stirring constantly to ensure that the paprika doesn't catch light and burn.

3 Add the potato slices to the skillet and cook them in a single layer for about 5 minutes or until they just begin to curl slightly at the edges.

4 Remove the potato slices from the skillet using a draining spoon.

5 Transfer the potato slices to paper towels and let them drain thoroughly.

6 Thread the potato slices on to several wooden kebab skewers.

7 Sprinkle the potato slices with a little salt and cook over a medium hot barbecue grill or under a medium broiler, turning frequently, for 10 minutes, until the potato slices begin to go crisp. Sprinkle with a little more salt, if preferred, and serve immediately.

SERVES 4

2 large potatoes
3 tbsp olive oil
½ tsp paprika
salt

NUTRITION

Calories *149*; Sugars *0.6 g*; Protein *2 g*;
Carbohydrate *17 g*; Fat *8 g*; Saturates *1 g*

⭐ very easy

🍳 5 mins

🕐 20 mins

COOK'S TIP

You could use curry powder or any other spice to flavor the chips instead of the paprika, if you prefer.

Fresh green beans have a wonderful flavor that is hard to beat. If you cannot find fresh beans, use thawed, frozen beans instead.

Mixed Bean Pan-Fry

S E R V E S   4

12 oz/350 g mixed fresh beans, such as green and fava beans, podded
2 tbsp vegetable oil
2 garlic cloves, crushed
1 red onion, halved and sliced
8 oz/225 g firm marinated bean curd, diced
1 tbsp lemon juice
½ tsp ground turmeric
1 tsp apple spice
⅔ cup Fresh Vegetable Bouillon (see page 16)
2 tsp sesame seeds

1 Trim, chop, and prepare the beans and set aside until required.

2 Heat the oil in a medium skillet. Add the garlic and onion and cook over low heat, stirring frequently, for 2 minutes. Add the bean curd and cook, stirring gently occasionally, for a further 2–3 minutes, until just beginning to turn golden brown.

3 Add the green beans and fava beans. Stir in the lemon juice, turmeric, apple spice, and vegetable stock and bring to a boil over medium heat.

4 Reduce the heat and simmer for about 5–7 minutes or until the beans are tender. Sprinkle with sesame seeds and serve immediately.

N U T R I T I O N
Calories *179*; Sugars *4 g*; Protein *10 g*;
Carbohydrate *10 g*; Fat *11 g*; Saturates *1 g*

⭐ very easy
🥄 10 mins
🕐 15 mins

👨‍🍳 **C O O K ' S   T I P**

Use smoked bean curd instead of marinated bean curd for an alternative and quite distinctive flavor.

Use large open-cap mushrooms for this recipe for their flavor and suitability for filling.

Stuffed Mushrooms

1 Remove the stems from the mushrooms and chop finely. Reserve the caps.

2 Heat the olive oil in a large, heavy skillet over a medium heat. Add the chopped mushroom stems, leek, celery, bean curd, zucchini, and carrot and cook, stirring constantly, for 3–4 minutes.

3 Stir in the bread crumbs, chopped basil, tomato paste, and pine nuts. Season with salt and pepper to taste and mix thoroughly.

4 Spoon the mixture into the mushroom caps and top with the grated cheese.

5 Place the mushrooms in a shallow casserole and pour the vegetable bouillon around them.

6 Cook in a preheated oven, 425°F/220°C, for 20 minutes, or until cooked through and the cheese has melted. Remove the mushrooms from the casserole and serve immediately with a salad.

SERVES 4

8 open-cap mushrooms
1 tbsp olive oil
1 small leek, chopped
1 celery stalk, chopped
3½ oz/100 g firm bean curd, diced
1 zucchini, chopped
1 carrot, chopped
scant 2 cups whole-wheat bread crumbs
2 tbsp chopped fresh basil
1 tbsp tomato paste
2 tbsp pine nuts
¾ cup grated colby cheese
⅔ cup Fresh Vegetable Bouillon
    (see page 16)
salt and pepper
salad, to serve

NUTRITION
Calories 273; Sugars 5 g; Protein 13 g;
Carbohydrate 15 g; Fat 18 g; Saturates 5 g

very easy

15 mins

25 mins

This imaginative and attractive recipe for artichokes stuffed with nuts, tomatoes, olives, and mushrooms, has been adapted for the microwave.

Stuffed Globe Artichokes

SERVES 4

4 globe artichokes
8 tbsp water
4 tbsp lemon juice
1 onion, chopped
1 garlic clove, crushed
2 tbsp olive oil
2 cups white mushrooms, chopped
1/2 cup pitted black olives, sliced
2 oz/55 g sun-dried tomatoes in oil, drained and chopped
1 tbsp chopped fresh basil
1 cup fresh white bread crumbs
1/4 cup pine nuts, toasted
oil from the jar of sun-dried tomatoes for drizzling
salt and pepper

NUTRITION
Calories 248; Sugars 8 g; Protein 5 g; Carbohydrate 16 g; Fat 19 g; Saturates 2 g

easy
30 mins
30-35 mins

1 Cut the stalks and lower leaves off the artichokes. Snip off the leaf tips with scissors. Place 2 artichokes in a large bowl with half the water and half the lemon juice. Cover and cook in the microwave, on HIGH power for 10 minutes, turning the artichokes over halfway through, until a leaf pulls away easily from the base. Let stand, covered, for 3 minutes before draining. Turn the artichokes upside down and let cool. Repeat to cook the remaining artichokes.

2 Place the onion, garlic, and olive oil in a bowl. Cover and cook on HIGH power for 2 minutes, stirring once. Add the mushrooms, olives, and sun-dried tomatoes. Cover and cook on HIGH power for 2 minutes.

3 Stir in the basil, bread crumbs, and pine nuts. Season the mixture to taste with salt and pepper.

4 Turn the artichokes the right way up and carefully pull the leaves apart. Remove the purple-tipped central leaves. Using a teaspoon, scrape out the hairy choke and discard.

5 Divide the stuffing into 4 equal portions and spoon into the center of each artichoke. Push the leaves back around the stuffing.

6 Arrange the stuffed artichokes in a shallow dish and drizzle over a little oil from the jar of sun-dried tomatoes. Cook on HIGH power for 7–8 minutes to reheat, turning the artichokes around halfway through.

Fennel has a wonderful anise flavor which is ideal for broiling or cooking on a barbecue. This marinated recipe is really delicious.

Marinated Fennel

1 Cut off and reserve the fennel fronds for the garnish. Cut each of the bulbs into 8 pieces and place in a shallow dish. Add the bell pepper and mix well.

2 To make the marinade, combine the lime juice, olive oil, garlic, mustard, and thyme. Pour the marinade over the fennel and bell pepper and toss to coat thoroughly. Cover with plastic wrap and set aside to marinate for 1 hour.

3 Thread the fennel and bell pepper onto presoaked wooden skewers, alternating with the lime wedges. Cook the kebabs under a preheated medium broiler, turning and basting frequently with the marinade, for about 10 minutes. Alternatively, cook on a medium hot barbecue, turning and basting frequently, for about 10 minutes.

4 Transfer the kebabs to serving plates, garnish with fennel fronds, and serve immediately with a crisp salad.

SERVES 4

2 fennel bulbs
1 red bell pepper, halved, seeded and cut into large dice
1 lime, cut into 8 wedges

marinade

2 tbsp lime juice
4 tbsp olive oil
2 garlic cloves, crushed
1 tsp wholegrain mustard
1 tbsp chopped thyme
fennel fronds, to garnish
crisp salad greens, to serve

NUTRITION
Calories 117; Sugars 3 g; Protein 1 g;
Carbohydrate 3 g; Fat 11 g; Saturates 2 g

⭐ very easy
🍽 1 hr 15 mins
🕐 10 mins

COOK'S TIP

Soak the skewers in cold water for 20 minutes before using to prevent them from burning during broiling. You could substitute 2 tablespoons of orange juice for the lime juice and add 1 tablespoon of honey, if you prefer.

This is so simple to prepare and looks great if you use a variety of mushrooms for shape and texture.

Garlic Mushrooms *on* Toast

S E R V E S   4

3 tbsp margarine
2 garlic cloves, crushed
¾ lb/350 g mixed mushrooms, such as open-cap, white, oyster, and shiitake, sliced
8 slices French stick
1 tbsp chopped fresh parsley
salt and pepper

1 Melt the margarine in a skillet. Add the crushed garlic and cook, stirring constantly, for 30 seconds.

2 Add the mushrooms and cook, turning occasionally, for 5 minutes.

3 Toast the French stick slices under a preheated medium broiler for 2–3 minutes, turning once. Transfer the toasts to a serving plate.

4 Toss the parsley into the mushrooms, mixing well, and season well with salt and pepper to taste.

5 Spoon the mushroom mixture over the bread and serve immediately.

N U T R I T I O N
Calories *366*; Sugars *2 g*; Protein *9 g*;
Carbohydrate *45 g*; Fat *18 g*; Saturates *4 g*

⊗   very easy
◔   10 mins
◷   10 mins

Omelets are very versatile: they go with almost anything and you can also serve them at any time of the day.

Indian-Style Omelet

1 Place the onion, chiles, and cilantro in a large mixing bowl and combine.

2 Whisk the eggs in a separate bowl. Stir the onion mixture into the eggs. Add the salt and whisk again.

3 Heat 1 tablespoon of the oil in a large, heavy skillet over a medium heat. Place a ladleful of the omelet batter in the pan. Cook the omelet, turning once and pressing down with a flat spoon to make sure that the egg is cooked right through, until the omelet is just firm and golden brown in color.

4 Repeat the same process with the remaining batter. Set the omelets aside, as you make them, and keep warm while you make the remaining batches.

5 Serve the omelets hot, garnished with fresh basil sprigs and accompanied by toasted bread. Alternatively, simply serve the omelets with crisp salad greens for a light lunch.

SERVES 4

1 small onion, chopped very finely
2 fresh green chiles, seeded and chopped finely
2 tbsp finely chopped fresh cilantro leaves
4 eggs
1 tsp salt
2 tbsp vegetable oil
fresh basil sprigs, to garnish
toasted bread or crisp salad greens, to serve

NUTRITION
Calories 132; Sugars 1 g; Protein 7 g; Carbohydrate 2 g; Fat 11 g; Saturates 2 g

easy

10 mins

20 mins

👨‍🍳 **COOK'S TIP**

All eggs are susceptible to bacteria. Store them in the refrigerator, with the pointed end downward, for up to 2 weeks, and never use cracked or dirty eggs. Bring them to room temperature about 30 minutes before using.

These tasty and attractive individual tartlets are great served hot at lunchtime or cool for picnic food.

Cress *and* Cheese Tartlets

SERVES 4

generous ¾ cup all-purpose flour,
    plus extra for dusting
pinch of salt
6 tbsp butter or margarine
2–3 tbsp cold water
2 bunches of arugula
2 garlic cloves, crushed
1 shallot, chopped
1¼ cups grated colby cheese
4 tbsp plain yogurt
½ tsp paprika

1 Strain the flour into a mixing bowl and add the salt. Rub 2 tablespoons of the butter or margarine into the flour until the mixture resembles bread crumbs. Stir in enough of the cold water to make a smooth dough.

2 Roll the dough out on a lightly floured counter and use to line four 4-inch/10-cm tartlet pans. Prick the bottoms of the tartlet shells with a fork and let chill in the refrigerator.

3 Heat the remaining butter or margarine in a skillet. Discard the stems from the arugula. Add the leaves to the pan with the garlic and shallot and cook for 1–2 minutes until wilted.

4 Remove the pan from the heat and stir in the grated colby cheese, yogurt, and paprika.

5 Spoon the mixture into the tartlet shells and cook in a preheated oven, 350°F/180°C, for 20 minutes or until the filling is just firm. Turn out the tartlets and serve immediately, if serving hot. If serving cold, place on a wire rack to cool, then store in the refrigerator until required.

NUTRITION
Calories *410*; Sugars *4 g*; Protein *15 g*;
Carbohydrate *24 g*; Fat *29 g*; Saturates *19 g*

moderate

20 mins

25 mins

🎩 **COOK'S TIP**

Use spinach instead of the arugula, making sure it is well drained before mixing with the remaining filling ingredients.

These are a delicious addition to any party buffet, and very simple to prepare. Serve with a sweet chile sauce.

Sweetcorn Patties

1 Mash the drained corn kernels lightly in a medium-sized bowl. Add the onion, curry powder, garlic, ground coriander, scallions, flour, baking powder, and egg. Stir well to combine thoroughly and season to taste with salt.

2 Heat the sunflower oil in a skillet. Drop tablespoonfuls of the mixture carefully into the hot oil, far enough apart for them not to run into each other as they cook.

3 Cook for about 4–5 minutes, turning each patty once, until they are golden brown and firm to the touch. Take care not to turn them too soon, or they will break up in the skillet.

4 Carefully remove the patties from the skillet with a slice and drain them well on absorbent paper towels. Serve immediately while still warm.

SERVES 4

1½ cups canned corn kernels, drained
1 onion, finely chopped
1 tsp curry powder
1 garlic clove, crushed
1 tsp ground coriander
2 scallions, chopped
3 tbsp all-purpose flour
½ tsp baking powder
1 large egg
4 tbsp sunflower oil
salt

NUTRITION
Calories 90; Sugars 3 g; Protein 2 g;
Carbohydrate 11 g; Fat 5 g; Saturates 0.6 g

⭐⭐ easy
🕐 10 mins
🕐 10 mins

👨‍🍳 **COOK'S TIP**

To make this dish more attractive, you can serve the patties on large leaves, like those shown in the photograph. Be sure to cut the scallions on the diagonal, as shown, for a more elegant appearance.

This substantial version of cheese on toast—a creamy cheese sauce topped with a poached egg—makes a tasty, filling snack.

Buck Rarebit

SERVES 4

3 cups grated sharp colby cheese
1 cups grated Dutch or Swiss cheese
1 tsp mustard powder
1 tsp whole-grain mustard
2–4 tbsp beer (Guinness), cider, or milk
½ tsp vegetarian Worcestershire sauce
4 thick slices white or whole-wheat bread
4 eggs
salt and pepper

to garnish
tomato wedges
arugula sprigs

1 Combine the cheeses and place in a nonstick pan.

2 Add the mustards, seasoning, beer, and the vegetarian Worcestershire sauce and mix well.

3 Heat the cheese mixture gently, stirring until it has melted and is completely thick and creamy. Remove from the heat and let cool a little.

4 Toast the slices of bread on one side of each side under a preheated broiler then spread the rarebit mixture evenly over 1 side of each piece. Put under a moderate broiler until golden brown and bubbling.

5 Meanwhile, poach the eggs. If using a poacher, grease the cups, heat the water in the pan and, when just boiling, break the eggs into the cups. Cover and simmer for 4–5 minutes until just set. Alternatively, bring about 1½ inches/4 cm of water to a boil in a skillet or large pan and for each egg quickly swirl the water with a knife and drop the egg into the "hole" created. Cook for about 4 minutes until just set.

6 Top the rarebits with a poached egg and serve garnished with tomato wedges and sprigs of arugula.

NUTRITION
Calories *478*; Sugars *2 g*; Protein *29 g*;
Carbohydrate *14 g*; Fat *34 g*; Saturates *20 g*

⭐ very easy

🕐 10 mins

🕐 15–20 mins

👨‍🍳 **COOK'S TIP**

For a change, you can use part or all Stilton or other blue cheese; the appearance is not so attractive but the flavor is very good.

These mildly spiced croquettes are an ideal light lunch served with a crisp salad and a sesame dip.

Lentil Croquettes

1 Put the lentils in a large pan with the bell pepper, onion, garlic, garam masala, chili powder, ground cumin, lemon juice, and peanuts. Add the water and bring to a boil. Reduce the heat and simmer gently, stirring occasionally, for about 30 minutes or until all the liquid has been absorbed.

2 Remove the mixture from the heat and let cool slightly. Beat in the egg and season to taste with salt and pepper. Let cool completely.

3 With floured hands, form the mixture into 8 rectangles or ovals.

4 Combine the flour, turmeric, and chili powder on a small plate. Roll the croquettes in the spiced flour mixture to coat thoroughly.

5 Heat the oil in a large skillet. Add the croquettes, in batches, and cook, turning once, for about 10 minutes until crisp on both sides. Transfer to warmed serving plates and serve the croquettes immediately with crisp salad greens and fresh herbs.

SERVES 4

1 cup split red lentils, washed
1 green bell pepper, halved, seeded, and chopped finely
1 red onion, chopped finely
2 garlic cloves, crushed
1 tsp garam masala
$\frac{1}{2}$ tsp chili powder
1 tsp ground cumin
2 tsp lemon juice
2 tbsp chopped unsalted peanuts
2$\frac{1}{2}$ cups water
1 egg, beaten
3 tbsp all-purpose flour
1 tsp ground turmeric
1 tsp chili powder
4 tbsp vegetable oil
salt and pepper
salad greens and fresh herbs, to serve

NUTRITION
Calories 409; Sugars 5 g; Protein 19 g;
Carbohydrate 48 g; Fat 17 g; Saturates 2 g

easy
40 mins
50 mins

These appetizing little patties, packed with creamy potato and a variety of mushrooms, make a quick and satisfying snack.

Mixed Mushroom Patties

SERVES 4

1 lb/450 g diced mealy potatoes
2 tbsp butter
2 cups chopped mixed mushrooms
2 garlic cloves, crushed
1 small egg, beaten
1 tbsp chopped fresh chives, plus extra
   to garnish
flour, for dusting
vegetable oil, for frying
salt and pepper
salad greens, to serve

1 Cook the potatoes in a pan of lightly salted boiling water for 10 minutes or until cooked through.

2 Drain the potatoes well, mash with a potato masher or fork, and set aside.

3 Meanwhile, melt the butter in a skillet. Add the mushrooms and garlic and cook over medium heat, stirring constantly, for 5 minutes. Drain well.

4 Stir the mushrooms and garlic into the potatoes, together with the beaten egg and chives.

5 Divide the mixture equally into 4 portions and shape them into round patties. Toss them in the flour until the outsides of the patties are completely coated, shaking off any excess.

6 Heat the vegetable oil in a skillet. Add the mushroom patties and cook over medium heat for 10 minutes until they are golden brown, turning them over carefully halfway through to prevent them breaking up. Serve the patties immediately, with a simple crisp salad.

NUTRITION
Calories 298; Sugars 0 .8g; Protein 5 g;
Carbohydrate 22 g; Fat 22 g; Saturates 5 g

easy

20 mins

25 mins

You can use dried garbanzo beans for this popular snack, but the canned sort are quick and easy without sacrificing much flavor.

Bombay Bowl

1 Drain the garbanzo beans and place them in a bowl.

2 Place the diced potatoes in a pan of water and boil until cooked through. Test by inserting the tip of a knife into the potatoes—they should feel soft and tender. Drain the potatoes and set them aside until required.

3 Mix together the tamarind paste and water in a small mixing bowl.

4 Add the chili powder, sugar, and salt to the tamarind paste mixture and stir well to combine. Pour the mixture over the garbanzo beans.

5 Add the chopped onion and the diced potatoes, and stir to mix. Season to taste with a little salt.

6 Transfer the mixture to a serving bowl and garnish with tomatoes, chiles, and cilantro leaves.

SERVES 4

1½ cups canned garbanzo beans
2 medium potatoes, diced
1 medium onion, chopped finely
2 tbsp tamarind paste
6 tbsp water
1 tsp chili powder
2 tsp sugar
1 tsp salt

to garnish
1 tomato, sliced
2 fresh green chiles, chopped
fresh cilantro leaves

NUTRITION
Calories *183*; Sugars *6 g*; Protein *9 g*;
Carbohydrate *33 g*; Fat *3 g*; Saturates *0.3 g*

⊘⊘ easy

◔ 15 mins

🕐 15 mins

🍴 **COOK'S TIP**

Cream-colored and resembling a filbert in appearance, garbanzo beans have a distinctive nutty flavor and slightly crunchy texture.

This dish is extremely versatile and could be made with any vegetables that you have to hand and basmati rice instead of brown.

Brown Rice Gratin

SERVES 4

½ cup brown rice
2 tbsp butter or margarine, plus extra
   for greasing
1 red onion, chopped
2 garlic cloves, crushed
1 carrot, cut into thin batons
1 zucchini, sliced
¾ cup baby corn ears, halved lengthwise
2 tbsp sunflower seeds
3 tbsp chopped fresh mixed herbs
1 cup grated mozzarella cheese
2 tbsp whole-wheat bread crumbs
salt and pepper

1 Cook the rice in a pan of lightly salted boiling water for 20 minutes until tender. Drain well.

2 Lightly grease a 3¾ cup casserole with butter or margarine.

3 Melt the butter or margarine in a skillet. Cook the onion over low heat, stirring, for 2 minutes or until soft.

4 Add the garlic, carrot, zucchini, and baby corn ears, and cook, stirring constantly, for a further 5 minutes until the vegetables are soft.

5 Combine the drained rice with the sunflower seeds and mixed herbs and stir into the skillet. Stir in half of the mozzarella cheese and season with salt and pepper to taste.

6 Spoon the mixture into the prepared casserole and top with the bread crumbs and remaining cheese.

7 Cook in a preheated oven, 350°F/ 180°C, for about 25–30 minutes or until the cheese has begun to turn golden. Serve immediately.

NUTRITION
Calories *321*; Sugars *6 g*; Protein *10 g*;
Carbohydrate *32 g*; Fat *18 g*; Saturates *9 g*

easy

15 mins

1 hr

These grated potato patties are also known as straw patties, as they resemble a straw mat! Serve them with a tomato sauce or salad.

Cheese *and* Onion Rostis

1 Parboil the potatoes in a pan of lightly salted boiling water for 10 minutes and let cool. Peel the potatoes, grate with a coarse grater, and place in a mixing bowl.

2 Stir in the onion, cheese, and parsley. Season well with salt and pepper. Divide the potato mixture into 4 portions of equal size and form them into patties.

3 Heat half of the olive oil and butter in a skillet. Cook 2 of the potato patties over high heat for 1 minute, then reduce the heat and cook for 5 minutes, until they are golden underneath. Turn them over and cook for another 5 minutes.

4 Repeat with the remaining oil and butter to cook the remaining patties. Transfer to warm individual serving plates. Garnish and serve immediately.

SERVES 4

2 lb/900 g potatoes
1 onion, grated
½ cup grated Swiss cheese
2 tbsp chopped fresh parsley
1 tbsp olive oil
2 tbsp butter
salt and pepper

to garnish
1 shredded scallion
1 small tomato, cut into fourths

COOK'S TIP

The potato patties should be flattened as much as possible during cooking, otherwise the outside will be cooked before the center.

NUTRITION
Calories *307*; Sugars *4 g*; Protein *8 g*;
Carbohydrate *42 g*; Fat *13 g*; Saturates *6 g*

easy

10 mins

40 mins

A hot cheese dip made from three different cheeses can be prepared easily and with guaranteed success in the microwave.

Three-Cheese Fondue

SERVES 4

1 garlic clove
1¼ cups dry white wine
2 cups grated mild colby cheese
1 cup grated Swiss cheese
1 cup grated mozzarella cheese
2 tbsp cornstarch
pepper

to serve

French stick, sliced
vegetables, such as zucchini, mushrooms,
	baby corn ears, and cauliflower

1 Bruise the garlic by placing the flat side of a knife on top and pressing down with the heel of your hand.

2 Rub the garlic around the inside of a large bowl. Discard the garlic.

3 Pour the wine into the bowl and heat, uncovered, on HIGH power for 3–4 minutes, until hot, but not boiling.

4 Gradually add the colby cheese and Swiss cheeses, stirring well after each addition (see Cook's Tip), then add the mozzarella. Stir until all the cheese is completely melted.

5 Mix the cornstarch with a little water to form a smooth paste and stir it into the cheese mixture. Season to taste with pepper.

6 Cover and cook on MEDIUM power for 6 minutes, stirring twice during cooking, until the sauce is smooth.

7 Cut the French stick into bite-sized cubes and the vegetables into batons, slices, or flowerets. To serve, keep the fondue warm over a spirit lamp or reheat as necessary in the microwave oven. Dip in cubes of French stick and batons, slices, or vegetable flowerets.

NUTRITION

Calories *565*; Sugars *1 g*; Protein *29 g*;
Carbohydrate *15 g*; Fat *38 g*; Saturates *24 g*

⊘ very easy

◔ 15 mins

◷ 10 mins

🍴 **COOK'S TIP**

Make sure you add the cheese to the wine gradually, mixing well in between each addition, to prevent the mixture from curdling.

This recipe takes a while to prepare, but it is well worth the effort. The golden potato slices coated in bread crumbs and cheese are delicious.

Cheese *and* Potato Slices

1 Cook the sliced potatoes in a pan of boiling water for about 10–15 minutes, or until they are just tender. Drain thoroughly.

2 Mix the bread crumbs, cheese, and chili powder together in a bowl, then transfer to a shallow dish. Pour the beaten eggs into a separate dish.

3 Dip the potato slices first in egg and then roll them in the bread crumbs to coat completely.

4 Heat the oil in a large pan to 350°F/180°C, or until a cube of bread browns in 30 seconds. Cook the cheese and potato slices, in several batches, for 4–5 minutes or until they are a golden brown color.

5 Remove the cheese and potato slices from the oil with a draining spoon and drain thoroughly on paper towels. Keep the cheese and potato slices warm while you cook the remaining batches.

6 Transfer the cheese and potato slices to warm individual serving plates. Dust lightly with chili powder, if using, and serve immediately.

COOK'S TIP

The cheese and potato slices may be coated in the bread crumb mixture in advance and then stored in the refrigerator, until ready to use.

SERVES 4

2 lb/900 g large waxy potatoes, unpeeled and sliced thickly
1 cup fresh white bread crumbs
½ cup grated Parmesan cheese
1½ tsp chili powder
2 eggs, beaten
oil, for deep frying
chili powder, for dusting (optional)

NUTRITION
Calories 560; Sugars 3 g; Protein 19 g; Carbohydrate 55 g; Fat 31 g; Saturates 7 g

easy

10 mins

40 mins

Pasta, Grains, *and* Legumes

Pasta is one of the most popular and versatile ingredients available, and it is both nourishing and satisfying. Fresh or dried pasta is made in a variety of flavors and colors, shapes and sizes, all of which work well with a number of vegetarian sauces. Pasta combines well with vegetables, herbs, nuts, and cheeses to provide scores of interesting and tasty meals. Noodles are also quick to cook and provide good basic food that can be dressed up in all kinds of different ways. Often flavored with oriental ingredients, the noodle recipes in this chapter are sure to liven up a vegetarian diet.

This pasta dish is baked in the oven and cut into slices for serving. It looks and tastes terrific and is perfect when you want to impress.

Tomato *and* Pasta Bake

SERVES 4

1 cup pasta shapes, such as penne or casareccia
1 tbsp olive oil
1 leek, chopped
3 garlic cloves, crushed
1 green bell pepper, halved, deseeded, and chopped
2 cups canned chopped tomatoes
2 tbsp chopped, pitted black olives
2 eggs, beaten
1 tbsp chopped fresh basil

tomato sauce

1 tbsp olive oil
1 onion, chopped
1 cup canned chopped tomatoes
1 tsp caster sugar
2 tbsp tomato paste
²/₃ cup Fresh Vegetable Bouillon (see page 16)
salt and pepper

NUTRITION

Calories *179*; Sugars *6 g*; Protein *8 g*;
Carbohydrate *16 g*; Fat *10 g*; Saturates *3 g*

★★★ moderate
🕐 10 mins
🕐 1 hr 5 mins

1 Cook the pasta in a pan of boiling salted water for 8 minutes. Drain thoroughly.

2 Meanwhile, heat the olive oil in a pan and sauté the leek and garlic for 2 minutes, stirring constantly. Add the pepper, tomatoes, and olives to the pan and cook for a further 5 minutes.

3 Remove the pan from the heat and stir in the pasta, beaten eggs, and basil. Season well, and spoon into a lightly greased 2 pint/1 liter heatproof bowl.

4 Place the bowl in a roasting pan and half-fill the pan with boiling water. Cover the bowl, and cook in a preheated oven, 350°F/180°C, for 40 minutes, until set.

5 To make the sauce, heat the olive oil in a pan and sauté the onion for 2 minutes. Add the remaining ingredients to the pan and cook for a further 10 minutes. Put the sauce in a food processor or blender and blend until smooth. Return to a clean pan and heat through again until hot.

6 Turn the pasta out of the bowl onto a warm plate. Slice and serve with the tomato sauce.

This dish is made with prepared cannelloni tubes, but may also be made by rolling ready-bought lasagna sheets.

Vegetable Cannelloni

1 Heat the oil in a skillet. Add the eggplant and cook over moderate heat, stirring frequently, for 2–3 minutes.

2 Add the spinach, garlic, cumin, and mushrooms and reduce the heat. Season to taste with salt and pepper and cook, stirring constantly, for 2–3 minutes. Spoon the mixture into the cannelloni tubes and arrange in a casserole in a single layer.

3 To make the sauce, heat the olive oil in a pan and cook the onion and garlic for 1 minute. Add the tomatoes, sugar, and basil and bring to a boil. Reduce the heat and simmer gently for about 5 minutes. Spoon the sauce over the cannelloni tubes.

4 Arrange the sliced mozzarella on top of the sauce and cook in a preheated oven, 375°F/190°C, for about 30 minutes or until the cheese is bubbling and golden brown. Serve immediately.

SERVES 4

1 eggplant, diced
½ cup olive oil
8 oz/225 g spinach
2 garlic cloves, crushed
1 tsp ground cumin
1¼ cups chopped mushrooms
12 cannelloni tubes
salt and pepper

tomato sauce

1 tbsp olive oil
1 onion, chopped
2 garlic cloves, crushed
4 cups canned chopped tomatoes
1 tsp superfine sugar
2 tbsp chopped fresh basil
½ cup sliced mozzarella

NUTRITION
Calories *594*; Sugars *12 g*; Protein *13 g*;
Carbohydrate *52 g*; Fat *38 g*; Saturates *7 g*

⭐⭐⭐ moderate

🌓 30 mins

🕐 45 mins

This colorful and tasty lasagna has layers of sliced eggplants and vegetables in tomato sauce, all topped with a rich cheese sauce.

Vegetable Lasagna

SERVES 4

1 eggplant, sliced
3 tbsp olive oil
2 garlic cloves, crushed
1 red onion, halved and sliced
3 mixed bell peppers, diced
8 oz/225 g mixed mushrooms, sliced
2 celery stalks, sliced
1 zucchini, diced
½ tsp chili powder
½ tsp ground cumin
2 tomatoes, chopped
1¼ cups crushed tomatoes
2 tbsp chopped fresh basil
8 precooked lasagna verde sheets
salt and pepper

cheese sauce

2 tbsp butter
1 tbsp flour
⅔ cup Fresh Vegetable Bouillon
1⅓ cups milk
¾ cup grated colby cheese
1 tsp Dijon mustard
1 tbsp chopped basil
1 egg, beaten

NUTRITION

Calories *544*; Sugars *18 g*; Protein *20 g*;
Carbohydrate *61 g*; Fat *26 g*; Saturates *12 g*

⭐⭐⭐   moderate
🕐   35 mins
🕐   55 mins

1 Place the eggplant slices in a colander, sprinkle them with salt, and let stand for 20 minutes. Rinse under cold water, drain, and reserve.

2 Heat the oil in a pan and sauté the garlic and onion for 1–2 minutes. Add the bell peppers, mushrooms, celery, and zucchini and cook, stirring constantly, for 3–4 minutes.

3 Stir in the spices and cook for 1 minute. Mix in the chopped tomatoes, crushed tomatoes, and basil and season to taste with salt and pepper.

4 For the sauce, melt the butter in a pan, stir in the flour, and cook for 1 minute. Remove from the heat, stir in the bouillon and milk, return to the heat, and add half the cheese and all the mustard. Boil, stirring, until thickened. Stir in the basil. Remove from the heat and stir in the egg.

5 Place half the lasagna sheets in an ovenproof dish. Top with half the vegetable mixture then half the eggplants. Repeat the layers and spoon the cheese sauce over the top.

6 Sprinkle the lasagna with the remaining cheese and cook in a preheated oven, 350°F/180°C, for 40 minutes, until the top is golden brown.

Use any pasta shapes that you have for this recipe—fusilli were used here. Multicolored pasta is visually the most attractive to use.

Spinach *and* Nut Pasta

1 Bring a large pan of lightly salted water to a boil. Add the pasta, bring back to a boil, and cook for 8–10 minutes until the pasta is tender, but still firm to the bite. Drain well.

2 Meanwhile, heat the oil in a large pan. Add the garlic and onion and cook over a low heat, stirring occasionally, for 1 minute.

3 Add the sliced mushrooms to the pan and cook over a medium heat, stirring occasionally, for 2 minutes.

4 Lower the heat, add the spinach, and cook, stirring occasionally, for about 4–5 minutes or until the spinach has just wilted.

5 Stir in the pine nuts and wine, season to taste with salt and pepper, and cook for 1 minute.

6 Transfer the pasta to a warm serving bowl and toss the sauce into it, mixing well. Garnish with shavings of Parmesan cheese and serve immediately.

SERVES 4

2 cups dried pasta shapes
½ cup olive oil
2 garlic cloves, crushed
1 onion, cut into fourths and sliced
3 large flat mushrooms, sliced
8 oz/225 g spinach
2 tbsp pine nuts
5 tbsp dry white wine
salt and pepper
Parmesan shavings, to garnish

NUTRITION

Calories *603*; Sugars *5 g*; Protein *12 g*; Carbohydrate *46 g*; Fat *41 g*; Saturates *6 g*

⭐ very easy
🍳 5 mins
🕐 15 mins

🎩 **COOK'S TIP**

Grate a little nutmeg over the dish for extra flavor, because this spice has a particular affinity with spinach.

This dish is considered the Thai national dish, as it is made and eaten everywhere—a one-dish, fast food for eating on the move.

Thai-style Stir-Fried Noodles

SERVES 4

½ lb dried rice noodles
2 red chiles, seeded and chopped finely
2 shallots, chopped finely
2 tbsp sugar
2 tbsp tamarind water
1 tbsp lime juice
2 tbsp light soy sauce
1 tbsp sunflower oil
1 tsp sesame oil
6 oz/175 g diced smoked bean curd
pepper
2 tbsp chopped roasted peanuts, to garnish

1 Cook the rice noodles as directed on the pack, or soak them in boiling water for 5 minutes.

2 Grind together the chiles, shallots, sugar, tamarind water, lime juice, light soy sauce, and pepper to taste.

3 Heat the sunflower and sesame oils together in a preheated wok or large, heavy skillet over high heat. Add the bean curd and stir-fry for 1 minute.

4 Add the chile mixture, bring to a boil, and continue to cook, stirring constantly, for about 2 minutes, until the sauce has thickened.

5 Drain the rice noodles and add them to the chile mixture. Use 2 spoons to lift and stir the noodles until they are no longer steaming.

6 Serve the hot noodles immediately, garnished with the chopped peanuts.

NUTRITION
Calories 407; Sugars 11 g; Protein 14 g;
Carbohydrate 56 g; Fat 16 g; Saturates 3 g

⭐ very easy
🍳 15 mins
🕐 8 mins

👨‍🍳 **COOK'S TIP**

This is a quick one-dish meal that is very useful if you are catering for a single vegetarian in the family.

This quick dish is an ideal lunchtime meal, packed with mixed mushrooms in a sweet sauce.

Stir-Fried Japanese Noodles

1 Place the Japanese egg noodles in a large bowl. Pour over enough boiling water to cover and let the noodles soak for 10 minutes.

2 Meanwhile, heat the sunflower oil in a large preheated wok.

3 Add the red onion and garlic to the wok and cook for 2–3 minutes, or until they are soft.

4 Add the mushrooms to the wok and cook for about 5 minutes, or until the mushrooms have softened.

5 Drain the soaked egg noodles thoroughly.

6 Add the bok choi, drained noodles, sweet sherry, and bouillon to the wok.

7 Toss all of the ingredients together and cook for 2–3 minutes or until the liquid is just bubbling.

8 Transfer the mushroom noodles to warm serving bowls and scatter with sliced scallions and toasted sesame seeds. Serve immediately.

SERVES 4

½ lb/225 g Japanese egg noodles
2 tbsp sunflower oil
1 red onion, sliced
1 garlic clove, crushed
1 lb/450 g mixed mushrooms (shiitake, oyster, brown cap)
¾ lb/350 g bok choi
2 tbsp sweet sherry
6 tbsp Fresh Vegetable Bouillon (see pages 16)
4 scallions, sliced
1 tbsp toasted sesame seeds

NUTRITION
Calories 379; Sugars 8 g; Protein 12 g; Carbohydrate 53 g; Fat 13 g; Saturates 3 g

⭐⭐ easy
🕐 15 mins
🕐 20-25 mins

🍴 **COOK'S TIP**

The variety of mushrooms in large food stores has improved and a good mixture should be easily obtainable. If not, use the more common white and flat mushrooms.

In this simple recipe, cooked rice is pan-fried with vegetables and cashew nuts. It can either be eaten on its own or served as an accompaniment.

Special Fried Rice

SERVES 4

1 cup long grain rice
½ cup cashew nuts
2 tbsp vegetable oil
1 carrot, halved lengthwise and sliced
½ cucumber, halved, deseeded, and sliced
1 yellow bell pepper, halved, deseeded, and sliced
2 scallions, chopped
1 garlic clove, crushed
1 cup frozen peas, thawed
1 tbsp soy sauce
1 tsp salt
fresh cilantro leaves, to garnish

1 Bring a large pan of water to a boil. Add the rice to the pan and simmer for 15 minutes. Tip the rice into a strainer and rinse; drain thoroughly.

2 Heat a wok or large, heavy skillet, add the cashew nuts, and dry-fry, stirring constantly, until lightly browned. Remove and set aside.

3 Heat the oil in a wok or large skillet. Add the prepared vegetables and the garlic. Stir-fry for 3 minutes. Add the rice, peas, soy sauce, and salt. Continue to stir-fry, until the vegetables are well mixed, and thoroughly heated.

4 Stir in the reserved cashew nuts. Transfer the rice to a warmed serving dish, garnish with the cilantro leaves, and serve immediately.

NUTRITION
Calories *355*; Sugars *6 g*; Protein *9 g*;
Carbohydrate *48 g*; Fat *15 g*; Saturates *3 g*

easy

10 mins

30 mins

🍽 **COOK'S TIP**

You can replace any of the vegetables in this recipe with others suitable for a stir-fry, and using leftover rice makes this a perfect last-minute dish.

Egg noodles are cooked and then stir-fried with a colorful variety of vegetables to make this well-known and ever-popular dish.

Chow Mein

1 Cook the egg noodles according to the packet instructions. Drain and rinse under cold running water until cool. Set aside.

2 Heat 3 tablespoons of the vegetable oil in a preheated wok or skillet. Add the onion and carrots and stir-fry for 1 minute, then add the mushrooms, snow peas, and cucumber, and stir-fry for an additional 1 minute.

3 Stir in the remaining vegetable oil and add the drained noodles, together with the spinach and beansprouts.

4 Blend together all the remaining ingredients and pour the mixture over the noodles and vegetables.

5 Stir-fry until the noodle mixture is thoroughly heated through, transfer to a warm serving dish, and serve.

SERVES 4

1 lb/450 g egg noodles
4 tbsp vegetable oil
1 onion, sliced thinly
2 carrots, cut into thin sticks
¼ lb/115 g white mushrooms, cut into fourths
1½ cups snow peas
½ cucumber, cut into sticks
¼ lb/115 g spinach, shredded
2 cups beansprouts
2 tbsp dark soy sauce
1 tbsp sherry
1 tsp salt
1 tsp sugar
1 tsp cornstarch
1 tsp sesame oil

NUTRITION
Calories *669*; Sugars *9 g*; Protein *19 g*; Carbohydrate *100 g*; Fat *23 g*; Saturates *4 g*

⭐ very easy
🕐 15 mins
🕐 10 mins

🍳 **COOK'S TIP**

For a spicy hot chow mein, add 1 tablespoon chile sauce or substitute chile oil for the sesame oil.

Baby spinach and fresh herbs are the basis of this colorful, refreshing risotto that tastes of summer.

Risotto Verde

SERVES 4

7½ cups Fresh Vegetable Bouillon (see page 16)
2 tbsp olive oil
2 garlic cloves, crushed
2 leeks, shredded
2 cups risotto rice
1¼ cups dry white wine
4 tbsp chopped fresh mixed herbs
½ lb/225 g young spinach
3 tbsp low-fat plain yogurt
salt and pepper
shredded leek, to garnish

NUTRITION
Calories 374; Sugars 5 g; Protein 10 g;
Carbohydrate 55 g; Fat 9 g; Saturates 2 g

moderate

5 mins

45 mins

1 Pour the bouillon into a large pan and bring to a boil, then reduce the heat to a simmer.

2 Meanwhile, heat the oil in a separate pan and cook the garlic and leeks, stirring occasionally, for 2–3 minutes, until soft, but not browned.

3 Stir in the rice and cook, stirring constantly, until translucent and well coated with oil.

4 Pour in half of the wine and a little of the hot bouillon; it will bubble and steam rapidly. Cook over gentle heat, stirring, until all of the liquid has been absorbed.

5 Gradually add the remaining bouillon and wine and cook over low heat for 25 minutes, stirring all the time or until the rice is creamy (see Cook's Tip).

6 Stir in the chopped mixed herbs and spinach, season to taste, and cook for a further 2 minutes.

7 Stir in the plain yogurt, garnish with the shredded leek, and serve the risotto immediately.

COOK'S TIP

Do not hurry the process of cooking the risotto as the rice must absorb the liquid slowly in order for it to reach the correct consistency.

An eggplant is halved and filled with a risotto mixture, topped with cheese, and baked to make a snack or quick meal for two.

Risotto *in* Shells

1 Cook the rice in boiling salted water for about 15 minutes, until just tender. Drain, rinse, and drain again.

2 Bring a large pan of water to a boil. Cut the stem off the eggplant and cut the eggplant in half lengthwise. Cut out the flesh from the center carefully, leaving about a ½-inch/1.5-cm shell. Blanch the shells in the boiling water for 3–4 minutes. Drain thoroughly, then chop the eggplant flesh finely.

3 Heat the olive oil in a pan or skillet. Add the onion and garlic and cook over low heat until beginning to soften, then add the bell pepper and eggplant flesh and continue cooking for 2–3 minutes. Add the water to the pan and cook for a further 2–3 minutes.

4 Remove the pan from the heat, stir the raisins, chopped cashew nuts, dried oregano, and cooked rice into the eggplant mixture, and season to taste with salt and pepper.

5 Place the eggplant shells in an ovenproof dish and spoon in the rice mixture, piling it up well. Cover and cook in a preheated oven, 375°F/190°C, for 20 minutes.

6 Remove the lid and sprinkle the grated colby cheese over the rice, covering it evenly. Place the dish under a preheated moderate broiler and cook for 3–4 minutes, until golden brown and bubbling. Serve hot, garnished with oregano or parsley.

SERVES 4

⅓ cup mixed long grain and wild rice
1 large eggplant
1 tbsp olive oil
1 small onion, chopped finely
1 garlic clove, crushed
½ small red bell pepper, halved, seeded, and chopped
2 tbsp water
¼ cup raisins
¼ cup cashew nuts, chopped roughly
½ tsp dried oregano
½ cup grated sharp colby or Parmesan cheese
salt and pepper
fresh oregano or parsley, to garnish

NUTRITION
Calories *444*; Sugars *20 g*; Protein *13 g*; Carbohydrate *50 g*; Fat *23 g*; Saturates *8 g*

✪✪✪   moderate

🕐   20 mins

🕐   55 mins

Cajun spices add a flavor of the Deep South to this colorful rice and red kidney bean salad.

Deep South Rice *and* Beans

SERVES 4

1 cup long grain rice
4 tbsp olive oil
1 small green bell pepper, halved, deseeded and chopped
1 small red bell pepper, halved, deseeded and chopped
1 onion, chopped finely
1 small red or green chile, seeded and chopped finely
2 tomatoes, chopped
1 cup canned red kidney beans, rinsed and drained
1 tbsp chopped fresh basil
2 tsp chopped fresh thyme
1 tsp Cajun spice
salt and pepper
fresh basil leaves, to garnish

1 Cook the rice in plenty of boiling, lightly salted water for about 12 minutes, until it is just tender. Rinse under cold water, drain well, and set aside.

2 Meanwhile, heat the olive oil in a skillet, add the green and red bell peppers, and the onion, and cook gently for about 5 minutes, until soft.

3 Add the chile and tomatoes and cook for a further 2 minutes.

4 Add the vegetable mixture and the drained red kidney beans to the cooked rice, and stir thoroughly, but gently, to combine.

5 Add the chopped fresh herbs and the Cajun spice to the rice mixture and stir again to combine.

6 Season the salad to taste with salt and pepper, and serve, garnished with fresh basil leaves.

NUTRITION
Calories *336*; Sugars *8 g*; Protein *7 g*;
Carbohydrate *51 g*; Fat *13 g*; Saturates *2 g*

⭐ very easy
🕐 10 mins
🕐 20 mins

The whole spices are not meant to be eaten and may be removed before serving. Omit the broccoli and mushrooms for a plain, spiced pilau.

Spiced Basmati Pilau

1 Place the rice in a strainer and wash well under cold running water. Drain. Trim off most of the broccoli stalk and cut into small flowerets, then quarter the stalk lengthwise and cut diagonally into ½-inch/1-cm pieces.

2 Heat the oil in a large pan. Add the onions and broccoli stalks and cook over low heat, stirring frequently, for 3 minutes. Add the mushrooms, rice, garlic, and spices and cook for 1 minute, stirring, until the rice is coated in oil.

3 Add the boiling bouillon and season to taste with salt and pepper. Stir in the broccoli flowerets and return the mixture to a boil. Cover, reduce the heat, and cook over low heat for 15 minutes without uncovering the pan.

4 Remove the pan from the heat and let the pilau stand for 5 minutes without uncovering. Remove the whole spices, add the raisins and pistachios, and gently fork through to fluff up the grains. Serve the pilau hot.

SERVES 4

2½ cups basmati rice
6 oz/175 g broccoli, trimmed
6 tbsp vegetable oil
2 large onions, chopped
½ lb sliced mushrooms
2 garlic cloves, crushed
6 cardamom pods, split
6 whole cloves
8 black peppercorns
1 cinnamon stick or piece of cassia bark
1 tsp ground turmeric
5 cups boiling Fresh Vegetable Bouillon (see page 16) or water
salt and pepper
⅓ cup seedless raisins
½ cup unsalted pistachios, chopped coarsely

NUTRITION

Calories *450*; Sugars *3 g*; Protein *9 g*; Carbohydrate *76 g*; Fat *15 g*; Saturates *2 g*

⭐⭐ easy

🕐 20 mins

🕐 20 mins

🍳 **COOK'S TIP**

For added richness, you could stir a tablespoonful of vegetable ghee through the rice mixture just before serving. A little diced red bell pepper and a few cooked peas forked through at step 4 add a colorful touch.

Every Thai meal has as its centerpiece a big bowl of steaming, fluffy Thai jasmine rice, to which salt should not be added.

Thai Jasmine Rice

SERVES 4

open pan method
1 generous cup Thai jasmine rice
4 cups water

absorption method
1 generous cup Thai jasmine rice
2 cups water

1 For the open pan method, rinse the rice in a strainer under cold running water and let drain.

2 Bring the water to a boil. Add the rice, stir once, and return to a medium boil. Cook, uncovered, for 8–10 minutes, until the rice is tender.

3 Drain thoroughly and fork through lightly before serving.

1 For the absorption method, rinse the rice under cold running water.

2 Put the rice and water into a pan and bring to a boil. Stir once and then cover the pan tightly. Lower the heat as much as possible. Cook the rice for 10 minutes, and let rest for a further 5 minutes.

3 Fork through lightly and serve the rice immediately.

NUTRITION
Calories *239*; Sugars *0 g*; Protein *5 g*; Carbohydrate *54 g*; Fat *2 g*; Saturates *0.6 g*

⊛   very easy
◔   5 mins
◷   10 mins

🍳 **COOK'S TIP**

Thai jasmine rice can be frozen. Freeze in a plastic sealed container. Frozen rice is ideal for stir-fry dishes, as the process seems to separate the grains.

Couscous is a semolina grain which is very quick and easy to cook, and it makes a pleasant change from rice or pasta.

Vegetable Couscous

1 Heat the oil in a large pan and cook the onion, carrot, and turnip for 3–4 minutes. Add the bouillon, bring to a boil, cover, and simmer for 20 minutes.

2 Meanwhile, put the couscous in a bowl and moisten with a little boiling water, stirring, until the grains have swollen and separated.

3 Add the tomatoes, zucchini, bell pepper, and green beans to the pan.

4 Stir the lemon peel into the couscous, add the turmeric, if using, and mix thoroughly. Put the couscous in a steamer and position it over the pan of vegetables. Simmer the vegetables, steaming the couscous at the same time for 8–10 minutes.

5 Pile the couscous onto warmed serving plates. Ladle the vegetables over the top, together with some of their cooking liquid.

6 Scatter the vegetable couscous with the chopped cilantro or parsley and serve at once, garnished with the flatleaf parsley sprigs.

SERVES 4

2 tbsp vegetable oil
1 large onion, chopped coarsely
1 carrot, chopped
1 turnip, chopped
2½ cups Fresh Vegetable Bouillon
  (see page 16)
1 scant cup couscous
2 tomatoes, peeled and cut into fourths
2 zucchini, chopped
1 red bell pepper, halved, seeded,
  and chopped
¾ cup green beans, chopped
grated peel of 1 lemon
pinch of ground turmeric, optional
1 tbsp finely chopped fresh cilantro
  or parsley
salt and pepper
fresh flatleaf parsley sprigs, to garnish

NUTRITION
Calories *280*; Sugars *13 g*; Protein *10 g*;
Carbohydrate *47 g*; Fat *7 g*; Saturates *1 g*

⭐⭐⭐   moderate
🕐   20 mins
🕐   40 mins

Bulgur is very easy to use and, as well as being full of nutrients, it is a delicious alternative to rice, having a distinctive nutty flavor.

Bulgur Pilau

SERVES 4

6 tbsp butter or margarine
1 red onion, halved and sliced
2 garlic cloves, crushed
2 cups bulgur
6 oz/175 g tomatoes, deseeded and chopped
½ cup baby corn ears, halved lengthwise
3 oz/85 g small broccoli flowerets
3¾ cups Fresh Vegetable Stock (see page 16)
2 tbsp honey
scant ½ cup golden raisins
½ cup pine nuts
½ tsp ground cinnamon
½ tsp ground cumin
salt and pepper
sliced scallions, to garnish

1 Melt the butter or margarine in a large flameproof casserole over medium heat. Add the onion and garlic and cook, stirring occasionally, for 2–3 minutes until softened, but not browned.

2 Add the bulgur, tomatoes, corn ears, broccoli flowerets, and vegetable bouillon and bring to a boil. Reduce the heat, cover, and simmer gently, stirring occasionally, for 15–20 minutes.

3 Stir in the honey, golden raisins, pine nuts, ground cinnamon, and cumin, and season with salt and pepper to taste, mixing well. Remove the casserole from the heat, and set aside, covered, for 10 minutes.

4 Spoon the bulgur pilau into a warmed serving dish. Garnish with thinly sliced scallions and serve the pilau immediately.

NUTRITION
Calories *637*; Sugars *25 g*; Protein *16 g*;
Carbohydrate *90 g*; Fat *26 g*; Saturates *11 g*

easy

15 mins

35–40 mins

🎩 **COOK'S TIP**

The dish is left to stand for 10 minutes so that the bulgur can finish cooking and the flavors of the ingredients will mingle.

Plain boiled rice is eaten by most people in India every day, but for entertaining, a more interesting rice dish, such as this, is served.

Pilau Rice

1 Rinse the rice twice under running water and set aside until required.

2 Heat the ghee in a pan. Add the cardamoms, cloves, and peppercorns to the pan and cook, stirring constantly, for about 1 minute.

3 Add the rice and stir-fry over medium heat for a further 2 minutes.

4 Add the salt, saffron, and water to the rice mixture and reduce the heat. Cover the pan and simmer over low heat until the water has been absorbed.

5 Transfer the pilau rice to a serving dish and serve hot.

SERVES 4

1 cup basmati rice
2 tbsp vegetable ghee
3 green cardamoms
2 whole cloves
3 peppercorns
½ tsp salt
½ tsp saffron
1¾ cups water

NUTRITION
Calories *265*; Sugars *0 g*; Protein *4 g*;
Carbohydrate *43 g*; Fat *10 g*; Saturates *6 g*

✪✪✪   moderate
🕐   15 mins
🕐   20 mins

🍳 **COOK'S TIP**

The most expensive of all spices, saffron strands are the stamens of a type of crocus. They give dishes a rich, golden color, as well as adding a distinctive, slightly bitter taste. Saffron is sold as a powder or strands.

Rice cooked with tomatoes and onions will add color to your table, especially when garnished with green chiles and cilantro.

Tomato Rice

SERVES 4

⅔ cup vegetable oil
2 medium onions, sliced
1 tsp onion seeds
1 tsp finely chopped fresh gingerroot
1 tsp crushed garlic
½ tsp ground turmeric
1 tsp chili powder
1½ tsp salt
2 cups canned tomatoes
2½ cups basmati rice
2½ cups water

to garnish
3 fresh green chiles, chopped finely
fresh cilantro leaves, chopped
3 hard-cooked eggs

1 Heat the oil in a heavy pan. Add the onions and fry over a moderate heat, stirring frequently, for 5 minutes until golden brown.

2 Add the onion seeds, ginger, garlic, turmeric, chili powder, and salt, stirring to combine.

3 Reduce the heat, add the tomatoes, and stir-fry for 10 minutes, breaking them up.

4 Add the rice to the tomato mixture, stirring gently to coat the rice completely. Stir in the water. Cover the pan and cook over low heat until the water has been absorbed and the rice is tender, but still has some bite.

5 Transfer the tomato rice to a warmed serving dish. Garnish with the finely chopped green chiles, cilantro leaves, and hard-cooked eggs. Serve the tomato rice immediately.

NUTRITION
Calories *866*; Sugars *7 g*; Protein *15 g*; Carbohydrate *106 g*; Fat *46 g*; Saturates *6 g*

easy
10 mins
35 mins

COOK'S TIP

Onion seeds are always used whole in Indian cooking. They are often used in pickles and often sprinkled over the top of nan breads. They have nothing to do with the vegetable, but look similar to the plant's seed, hence the name.

Fragrant basmati rice is cooked with porcini mushrooms, spinach, and pistachio nuts in this easy microwave recipe.

Spinach *and* Nut Pilau

1 Place the porcini mushrooms in a small bowl. Pour over the hot water and let soak for 30 minutes.

2 Place the onion, garlic, ginger, chile, and oil in a large bowl. Cover and cook on HIGH power for 2 minutes. Rinse the rice, then stir it into the bowl, together with the carrot. Cover and cook on HIGH power for 1 minute.

3 Strain and coarsely chop the mushrooms. Add the mushroom soaking liquid to the bouillon to make 1¾ cups. Pour onto the rice.

4 Stir in the mushrooms, cinnamon, cloves, saffron, and ½ teaspoon salt. Cover and cook on HIGH power for 10 minutes, stirring once. Let the mixture stand, covered, for 10 minutes.

5 Place the spinach in a large bowl. Cover and cook on HIGH power for 3½ minutes, stirring once. Drain well and chop the spinach coarsely.

6 Stir the spinach, pistachio nuts, and chopped cilantro into the rice.

7 Season to taste with salt and pepper and garnish with cilantro leaves. Serve immediately.

SERVES 4

⅓ oz dried porcini mushrooms
1¼ cups hot water
1 onion, chopped
1 garlic clove, crushed
1 tsp grated fresh gingerroot
½ fresh green chile, seeded and chopped
2 tbsp oil
1¼ cups basmati rice
1 large carrot, grated
¾ cup Fresh Vegetable Bouillon (see page 16)
½ tsp ground cinnamon
4 whole cloves
½ tsp saffron strands
½ lb/225 g fresh spinach, long stalks removed
½ cup pistachio nuts
1 tbsp chopped fresh cilantro
salt and pepper
fresh cilantro leaves, to garnish

NUTRITION
Calories *403*; Sugars *7 g*; Protein *10 g*; Carbohydrate *62 g*; Fat *15 g*; Saturates *2 g*

⭐ very easy
🕐 55 mins
🕐 15–20 mins

The traditional breakfast plate of kedgeree reputedly has its roots in this Indian flavored rice dish, adopted by British colonists.

Kitchouri

SERVES 4

2 tbsp vegetable ghee or butter
1 red onion, chopped finely
1 garlic clove, crushed
½ celery stalk, chopped finely
1 tsp turmeric
½ tsp garam masala
1 green chile, seeded and chopped finely
½ tsp cumin seeds
1 tbsp chopped cilantro
1 generous ½ cup basmati rice, rinsed under cold water
1 generous ½ cup green lentils
1¼ cups vegetable juice
2½ cups Fresh Vegetable Bouillon (see page 16)

1 Heat the ghee or butter in a large heavy pan. Add the onion, garlic, and celery to the pan and cook for about 5 minutes, until soft.

2 Add the turmeric, garam masala, chopped green chile, cumin seeds, and cilantro. Cook over moderate heat, stirring constantly, for about 1 minute, until fragrant.

3 Add the rice and lentils and cook for 1 minute, until the rice is translucent.

4 Pour the vegetable juice and bouillon into the pan and bring to a boil over medium heat.

5 Cover and simmer over low heat, stirring occasionally, for about 20 minutes, or until the lentils are cooked (they should be tender when pressed between two fingers). Transfer the kitchouri to a warmed serving dish and serve immediately.

NUTRITION
Calories *318*; Sugars *5 g*; Protein *12 g*;
Carbohydrate *48 g*; Fat *10 g*; Saturates *6 g*

easy
10 mins
30 mins

 COOK'S TIP

This is a versatile dish, and can be served as a great-tasting and satisfying one-pot meal. It can also be served as a winter lunch dish with tomatoes and yogurt.

Biryani originated in the North of India, and was a dish reserved for festivals. The vegetables are marinated in a yogurt-based marinade.

Vegetable Biryani

1 Cook the potato cubes, carrots, and okra in a pan of boiling salted water for 7–8 minutes. Drain well and place in a large bowl. Mix with the celery, mushrooms, and eggplant.

2 Mix the plain yogurt, ginger, grated onions, garlic, turmeric, and curry powder, and spoon over the vegetables. Let marinate in a cool place for at least 2 hours.

3 Heat the butter in a heavy skillet. Add the sliced onions to the skillet and cook over medium heat for 5–6 minutes, until they are soft and golden brown. Remove a few onions from the pan and reserve for the garnish.

4 Cook the rice in a large pan of boiling water for 7 minutes. Drain thoroughly and set aside.

5 Add the marinated vegetables to the onions and cook for 10 minutes.

6 Put half of the rice into a 8¾ cup/2 liter casserole dish. Spoon the vegetables on top and cover with the remaining rice.

7 Cover the dish and cook the biryani in a preheated oven, 375°F/190°C, for 20–25 minutes, or until the rice is tender and the biryani is heated through.

8 Spoon the biryani onto a warm serving plate. Garnish with the reserved onions and cilantro and serve.

SERVES 4

¾ lb/350 g cubed potato
¼ lb/100 g baby carrots
2 oz/55 g okra, thickly sliced
2 celery stalks, sliced
3 oz/85 g baby white mushrooms, halved
1 eggplant, halved and sliced
1¼ cups plain yogurt
1 tbsp grated fresh gingerroot
2 large onions, grated
4 garlic cloves, crushed
1 tsp turmeric
1 tbsp curry powder
2 tbsp butter
2 onions, sliced
1¼ cups basmati rice
chopped fresh cilantro, to garnish

NUTRITION
Calories *449*; Sugars *18 g*; Protein *12 g*;
Carbohydrate *79 g*; Fat *12 g*; Saturates *6 g*

✪✪✪   moderate
🕐   2 hrs 15 mins
🕐   1 hr

Aloo Chat is one of a variety of Indian foods served at any time of the day. The garbanzo beans need to be soaked overnight.

Aloo Chat

SERVES 4

1 cup garbanzo beans, soaked overnight in cold water and drained
1 dried red chile
1 lb/450 g waxy potatoes, boiled in their skins and peeled
1 tsp cumin seeds
2 tsp salt
1 tsp black peppercorns
½ tsp dried mint
½ tsp chili powder
½ tsp ground ginger
2 tsp mango powder
½ cup plain yogurt
oil, for deep frying
4 poppadoms

1 Boil the garbanzo beans with the chile in plenty of water for about 1 hour until tender, then drain.

2 Cut the potatoes into 1-inch/2.5-cm dice and mix into the garbanzo beans while they are still warm. Set aside.

3 Grind together the cumin seeds, salt, and peppercorns in a spice grinder or in a pestle and mortar. Stir in the mint, chili, ginger, and mango powder.

4 Put a small pan or skillet over a low heat and add the spice mix. Cook, stirring, until the spices give off their aroma and then immediately remove the pan from the heat.

5 Stir half of the spice mix into the garbanzo bean and potato mixture and stir the other half into the yogurt.

6 Cook the poppadoms according to the packet instructions. Drain on plenty of paper towels. Break into bite-size pieces and stir into the potatoes and garbanzo beans, spoon over the spiced yogurt, and serve immediately.

NUTRITION
Calories *262*; Sugars *6 g*; Protein *13 g*;
Carbohydrate *46 g*; Fat *4 g*; Saturates *0.5 g*

moderate
8 hrs 35 mins
1 hr 5 mins

COOK'S TIP

Instead of garbanzo beans, diced tropical fruits can be stirred into the potatoes and spice mix; add a little lemon juice to balance the sweetness.

This is just one version of many dhals that are served throughout India; as many people are vegetarian, dhals form a staple part of the diet.

Tarka Dhal

1 Heat half of the ghee in a large pan and add the shallots. Cook for 2–3 minutes over high heat, then add the mustard seeds. Cover the pan until the seeds begin to pop.

2 Immediately remove the lid from the pan and add the garlic, fenugreek, ginger, and salt.

3 Stir once and add the lentils, tomato paste, and water. Bring to a boil, then lower the heat and simmer gently for 10 minutes.

4 Stir in the tomatoes, lemon juice, and chopped cilantro and simmer for 4–5 minutes until the lentils are tender.

5 Transfer to a serving dish. Heat the remaining ghee in a pan. Remove from the heat and stir in the garam masala and chili powder. Pour over the tarka dhal and serve.

SERVES 4

2 tbsp ghee
2 shallots, sliced
1 tsp yellow mustard seeds
2 garlic cloves, crushed
8 fenugreek seeds
1 tsp grated fresh gingerroot
½ tsp salt
generous ½ cup red lentils, washed
1 tbsp tomato paste
2½ cups water
2 tomatoes, peeled and chopped
1 tbsp lemon juice
4 tbsp chopped fresh cilantro
½ tsp garam masala
½ tsp chili powder

NUTRITION
Calories *183*; Sugars *4 g*; Protein *8 g*; Carbohydrate *22 g*; Fat *8 g*; Saturates *5 g*

easy

10 mins

25 mins

🍲 **COOK'S TIP**

The flavors in a dhal can be altered to suit your particular taste; for example, for extra heat, add more chili powder or chiles, or add fennel seeds for a pleasant anise flavor.

Dried pulses and lentils can be cooked in similar ways, but the soaking and cooking times do vary, so check the packet for instructions.

Toovar Dhal

SERVES 6

2 tbsp vegetable ghee
1 large onion, chopped finely
1 garlic clove, crushed
1 tbsp grated fresh gingerroot
1 tbsp cumin seeds, ground
2 tsp coriander seeds, ground
1 dried red chile
1-inch/2.5-cm piece of cinnamon stick
1 tsp salt
½ tsp ground turmeric
1 cup split yellow peas, soaked in cold water
    for 1 hour and drained
2 cups canned plum tomatoes
1¼ cups water
2 tsp garam masala

1 Heat the ghee in a large pan, add the onion, garlic, and ginger and sauté for 3–4 minutes until the onion has softened slightly.

2 Add the cumin, coriander, chile, cinnamon, salt, and turmeric, then stir in the split peas until well mixed.

3 Add the tomatoes, with their can juices, breaking up the tomatoes slightly with the back of a spoon.

4 Add the water and bring to a boil. Reduce the heat to very low and simmer the split peas, uncovered, stirring occasionally, for about 40 minutes until most of the liquid has been absorbed and the split peas are tender. Skim the surface occasionally with a slotted spoon to remove any scum.

5 Gradually stir in the garam masala, tasting after each addition, until it is to your taste. Serve hot.

NUTRITION

Calories *195*; Sugars *4 g*; Protein *11 g*;
Carbohydrate *28 g*; Fat *5 g*; Saturates *3 g*

easy

1 hr 10 mins

50 mins

 COOK'S TIP

Use a nonslip pan if you have one, because the mixture is quite dense and does stick to the base of the pan occasionally. If the dhal is overstirred, the split peas will break up and the dish will not have much texture or bite.

Traditionally, koftas are made from a spicy meat mixture, but this bean and wheat version makes a tasty vegetarian alternative.

Kofta Kebabs

1 Cook the adzuki beans in boiling water for 40 minutes, until tender. Drain, rinse, and let cool. Cook the bulgur wheat in the bouillon for 10 minutes, until the bouillon is absorbed. Set aside.

2 Heat 1 tablespoon of the olive oil in a skillet and sauté the onion, garlic, and spices for 4–5 minutes.

3 Transfer to a bowl, together with the beans, cilantro, seasoning, and eggs and mash with a potato masher or fork. Add the bread crumbs and bulgur wheat and stir well to combine. Cover and chill for 1 hour, until firm.

4 To make the tabbouleh, soak the bulgur wheat in 1¾ cups of boiling water for 15 minutes or until all the water has been absorbed. Combine with the remaining ingredients, then cover and chill until required.

5 With wet hands, mold the kofta mixture into 32 oval shapes.

6 Press on to skewers, brush with oil, and broil for 5–6 minutes until golden. Turn, brush with oil again, and broil for 5–6 minutes. Drain on paper towels. Garnish and serve with the tabbouleh.

SERVES 4

1 cup adzuki beans
1 cup bulgur wheat
2 cups Fresh Vegetable Bouillon
  (see page 16)
3 tbsp olive oil, plus extra for brushing
1 onion, chopped finely
2 garlic cloves, crushed
1 tsp ground coriander
1 tsp ground cumin
2 tbsp chopped fresh cilantro
3 eggs, beaten
1 cup dried bread crumbs
salt and pepper

tabbouleh
1 cup bulgur wheat
2 tbsp lemon juice
1 tbsp olive oil
6 tbsp chopped fresh parsley
4 scallions, chopped finely
⅓ cup finely chopped cucumber
3 tbsp chopped fresh mint
1 extra-large tomato, finely chopped

NUTRITION
Calories *598*; Sugars *7 g*; Protein *26 g*;
Carbohydrate *90 g*; Fat *17 g*; Saturates *3 g*

⭐⭐⭐   moderate
🕐   1 hr 20 mins
🕐   1 hr 25 mins

Stir-fries *and* Sautés

Stir-frying is one of the most convenient and nutritious ways of cooking vegetarian food as ingredients are cooked quickly over a very high heat in very little oil. The high heat seals in the natural juices and helps preserve nutrients. The short cooking time makes the vegetables more succulent and preserves texture as well as the natural flavor and color. A round-bottomed wok is ideal for stir-frying as it conducts and retains heat evenly and requires the use of less oil. You need a flat-bottomed pan for sautéing so that the food can be easily tossed and stirred. A brisk heat is essential so that the food turns golden brown and crisp.

This colorful and interesting mixture of vegetables, cooked in a spicy sauce, is excellent served with rice and naan bread.

Vegetable Curry

SERVES 4

8 oz/225 g turnips or rutabaga
1 eggplant
12 oz/350 g new potatoes
8 oz/225 g cauliflower
8 oz/225 g white mushrooms
1 large onion
3 carrots
6 tbsp vegetable ghee or vegetable oil
2 garlic cloves, crushed
4 tsp finely chopped fresh gingerroot
1–2 fresh green chiles, seeded and chopped
1 tbsp paprika
2 tsp ground coriander
1 tbsp mild or medium curry powder or paste
2 cups Fresh Vegetable Bouillon (see page 16)
2 cups canned chopped tomatoes
1 green bell pepper, halved, deseeded
    and sliced
1 tbsp cornstarch
2/3 cup coconut milk
2–3 tbsp ground almonds
salt
fresh cilantro sprigs, to garnish

NUTRITION

Calories *421*; Sugars *20 g*; Protein *12 g*;
Carbohydrate *42 g*; Fat *24 g*; Saturates *3 g*

easy

10 mins

45 mins

1 Cut the turnips, eggplant, and potatoes into ½-inch/1-cm cubes. Divide the cauliflower into small florets. Leave the mushrooms whole or slice them thickly if preferred. Slice the onion and carrots.

2 Heat the ghee or oil in a large pan. Add the onion, turnip or rutabaga, potato, and cauliflower and cook over low heat, stirring frequently, for 3 minutes.

3 Add the garlic, ginger, chiles, paprika, ground coriander, and curry powder or paste and cook, stirring, for 1 minute.

4 Add the bouillon, tomatoes, eggplant, and mushrooms and season with salt. Cover and simmer, stirring occasionally, for about 30 minutes or until tender. Add the bell pepper and carrots, cover, and cook for 5 minutes.

5 Blend the cornstarch with the coconut milk to a smooth paste and stir into the mixture. Add the ground almonds and simmer, stirring constantly, for 2 minutes. Taste and adjust the seasoning if necessary. Transfer the curry to serving plates and serve hot, garnished with fresh cilantro sprigs.

Meat is very expensive in India and much of the population is vegetarian, so the cuisine is typified by tasty ways of cooking with vegetables.

Potato *and* Vegetable Curry

1 Heat the vegetable oil in a large heavy pan or skillet. Add the potato chunks, onions, and garlic and fry over low heat, stirring frequently, for 2–3 minutes until the onions are beginning to soften.

2 Add the garam masala, turmeric, ground cumin, ground coriander, ginger, and chile to the pan, mixing the spices into the vegetables, until they are well coated. Cook over low heat, stirring constantly, for 1 minute.

3 Add the cauliflower, tomatoes, peas, chopped fresh cilantro, and vegetable bouillon to the curry mixture.

4 Cook the potato curry over low heat for 30–40 minutes or until the potatoes are tender and completely cooked through.

5 Garnish the potato curry with fresh cilantro and serve with plain boiled rice or warm Indian bread.

SERVES 4

4 tbsp vegetable oil
8 oz/675 g waxy potatoes,
    cut into large chunks
2 onions, cut into fourths
3 garlic cloves, crushed
1 tsp garam masala
½ tsp ground turmeric
½ tsp ground cumin
½ tsp ground coriander
2 tsp grated fresh gingerroot
1 fresh red chile, chopped
2 cups cauliflower flowerets
4 tomatoes, peeled and cut into fourths
¾ cup frozen peas
2 tbsp chopped fresh cilantro
1¼ cups Fresh Vegetable Bouillon
    (see page 16)
shredded fresh cilantro, to garnish
boiled rice or warm Indian bread, to serve

NUTRITION
Calories *301*; Sugars *10 g*; Protein *9 g*;
Carbohydrate *41 g*; Fat *12 g*; Saturates *1 g*

easy

15 mins

40–45 mins

Paneer is a delicious fresh, soft cheese frequently used in Indian cooking. It is easily made at home, but must be made the day before it's required.

Muttar Paneer

SERVES 4

²/₃ cup vegetable oil
2 onions, chopped
2 garlic cloves, crushed
1 inch/2.5 cm piece of fresh gingerroot, chopped
1 tsp garam masala
1 tsp ground turmeric
1 tsp chili powder
1 lb/450 g frozen peas
1 cup canned chopped tomatoes
¹/₂ cup Fresh Vegetable Bouillon (see page 16)
salt and pepper
2 tbsp chopped fresh cilantro

paneer

11 cups milk
5 tbsp lemon juice
1 garlic clove, crushed (optional)
1 tbsp chopped cilantro (optional)

NUTRITION
Calories *550*; Sugars *25 g*; Protein *19 g*;
Carbohydrate *33 g*; Fat *39 g*; Saturates *12 g*

⭐⭐⭐   moderate
🕐   9 hrs 15 mins
🕐   30 mins

1 To make the paneer, bring the milk to a rolling boil in a large pan. Remove from the heat and stir in the lemon juice. Return to the heat for about 1 minute until the curds and whey separate. Remove from the heat. Line a strainer with a double thickness of cheesecloth and pour the mixture through the cheesecloth, adding the garlic and cilantro, if using. Squeeze all the liquid from the curds and let drain.

2 Transfer the cloth to a dish, cover with a plate and a heavy weight, and let stand overnight in the refrigerator.

3 Cut the pressed paneer into small cubes. Heat the oil in a large skillet. Add the paneer and cook until golden on all sides. Remove from the pan and drain on paper towels.

4 Pour off some of the oil, leaving about 4 tablespoons in the pan. Add the onions, garlic, and ginger and cook gently, stirring frequently, for 5 minutes. Stir in the spices and cook gently for 2 minutes. Add the peas, tomatoes, and bouillon, and season with salt and pepper. Cover and simmer, stirring occasionally, for 10 minutes, until the onion is tender.

5 Add the paneer cubes and continue to cook for a further 5 minutes. Taste and adjust the seasoning, if necessary. Sprinkle with the chopped cilantro and serve at once.

This vegetarian tomato curry is served topped with a few hard-cooked eggs. It is a lovely accompaniment to any Indian meal.

Tomato Curry

1 Place the tomatoes in a large mixing bowl. Add the ginger, garlic, chili powder, salt, ground coriander, and ground cumin and blend well.

2 Heat the vegetable oil in a pan. Add the onion seeds, mustard, fenugreek and white cumin seeds, and the dried red chilis, and stir-fry for about 1 minute, until they give off their aroma. Remove the pan from the heat.

3 Add the tomato mixture to the spicy oil mixture and return the pan to the heat. Stir-fry for about 3 minutes.

4 Reduce the heat and continue to cook, half covered with a lid, stirring frequently, for 7–10 minutes.

5 Sprinkle over 1 tablespoon of the lemon juice. Taste, and add the remaining lemon juice if required.

6 Transfer the tomato curry to a warmed serving dish, set aside, and keep warm until required.

7 Shell the hard-cooked eggs and cut them into quarters. Add them to the tomato curry, pushing them in gently, yolk end downward.

8 Garnish with the fresh cilantro leaves and serve hot.

SERVES 4

2 cups canned tomatoes
1 tsp chopped finely fresh gingerroot
1 tsp crushed garlic
1 tsp chili powder
1 tsp salt
$\frac{1}{2}$ tsp ground coriander
$\frac{1}{2}$ tsp ground cumin
4 tbsp vegetable oil
$\frac{1}{2}$ tsp onion seeds
$\frac{1}{2}$ tsp mustard seeds
$\frac{1}{2}$ tsp fenugreek seeds
pinch of white cumin seeds
3 dried red chilis
2 tbsp lemon juice
3 eggs, hard-cooked
fresh cilantro leaves

NUTRITION
Calories 170; Sugars 3 g; Protein 6 g;
Carbohydrate 3 g; Fat 15 g; Saturates 2 g

moderate

25 mins

15 mins

Green curry paste will keep for up to 3 weeks in the refrigerator. Serve the curry over rice or noodles.

Green Curry *with* Tempeh

SERVES 4

1 tbsp sunflower oil
6 oz/175 g marinated or plain bean curd
6 scallions, cut into 1-inch/2.5-cm pieces
²/₃ cup coconut milk
grated peel of 1 lime
¹/₂ oz/15 g fresh basil leaves
¹/₄ tsp liquid seasoning, such as Maggi

green curry paste

2 tsp coriander seeds
1 tsp cumin seeds
1 tsp black peppercorns
4 large fresh green chiles, seeded
2 shallots, cut into fourths
2 garlic cloves,
2 tbsp chopped fresh cilantro
grated peel of 1 lime
1 tbsp roughly chopped galangal
1 tsp ground turmeric
salt
2 tbsp oil
cilantro leaves, to garnish

NUTRITION

Calories *237*; Sugars *4 g*; Protein *16 g*;
Carbohydrate *5 g*; Fat *17 g*; Saturates *3 g*

⭐⭐⭐   moderate
🕐   20 mins
🕐   15–20 mins

1 To make the green curry paste, grind together the coriander, cumin seeds, and black peppercorns in a food processor or in a mortar with a pestle.

2 Blend the remaining ingredients together and add the ground spice mixture. The curry paste can be stored in a clean, dry jar for up to 3 weeks in the refrigerator, or it can be frozen in a suitable container.

3 Heat the oil in a wok or large, heavy skillet. Add the bean curd and stir over high heat for about 2 minutes until sealed on all sides. Add the scallions and stir-fry for 1 minute. Remove the bean curd and scallions and reserve.

4 Put half the coconut milk into the wok or skillet and bring to a boil. Add 6 tablespoons of the curry paste and the lime peel, and cook for 1 minute, until fragrant. Add the reserved bean curd and scallions to the wok or skillet.

5 Add the remaining coconut milk and simmer for about 7–8 minutes. Stir in the fresh basil leaves and liquid seasoning. Let the curry simmer for a further minute before serving, garnished with cilantro leaves.

This rice is really colorful and crunchy with the addition of corn kernels and red kidney beans.

Fried Rice *with* Spicy Beans

1 Heat the sunflower oil in a large preheated wok.

2 Add the onion and stir-fry over medium heat for about 2 minutes or until soft.

3 Lower the heat, add the rice, green bell pepper and chili powder, and stir-fry for 1 minute.

4 Pour in the boiling water. Bring back to a boil, then reduce the heat, and simmer for 15 minutes.

5 Stir in the corn kernels, kidney beans, and cilantro and heat through, stirring from time to time.

6 Transfer to a warmed serving bowl and serve hot, sprinkled with extra cilantro, if wished.

SERVES 4

3 tbsp sunflower oil

1 onion, finely chopped

generous 1 cup long grain rice

1 green bell pepper, halved, deseeded, and diced

1 tsp chili powder

2½ cups boiling water

¾ cup canned corn kernels

1 cup canned red kidney beans, drained and rinsed

2 tbsp chopped fresh cilantro, plus extra to garnish (optional)

NUTRITION

Calories *363*; Sugars *3 g*; Protein *10 g*; Carbohydrate *61 g*; Fat *11 g*; Saturates *2 g*

⭐⭐⭐   moderate

🕐   15 mins

🕐   20 mins

👩‍🍳 **COOK'S TIP**

For perfect fried rice, the raw rice should ideally be soaked in a bowl of water for a short time before cooking to remove excess starch. Short grain Asian rice can be substituted for the long grain rice.

This tasty meal is made with sliced potatoes, bean curd, and vegetables cooked in the skillet from which it is served.

Pan Potato Cake

SERVES 4

1½ lb/675 g waxy potatoes, unpeeled
    and sliced
1 carrot, diced
3 cups small broccoli flowerets
5 tbsp butter
2 tbsp vegetable oil
1 red onion, cut into fourths
2 garlic cloves, crushed
6 oz/175 g firm bean curd, diced
2 tbsp chopped fresh sage
¾ cup grated sharp cheese

1 Cook the sliced potatoes in a large pan of boiling water for 10 minutes. Drain thoroughly.

2 Meanwhile, cook the carrot and broccoli flowerets in a separate pan of boiling water for 5 minutes. Remove with a slotted spoon.

3 Heat the butter and oil in a 9-inch/23-cm skillet. Add the onion and garlic and fry over low heat for 2–3 minutes. Add half of the potato slices, covering the base of the skillet.

4 Cover the potato slices with the carrot, broccoli, and bean curd. Sprinkle with half of the sage and cover with the remaining potato slices. Sprinkle the grated cheese over the top.

5 Cook over medium heat for 8–10 minutes. Then place the skillet under a preheated broiler for 2–3 minutes, or until the cheese melts and browns.

6 Garnish with the remaining sage and serve immediately, straight from the skillet.

NUTRITION
Calories *452*; Sugars *6 g*; Protein *17 g*;
Carbohydrate *35 g*; Fat *28 g*; Saturates *13 g*

easy

15 mins

30 mins

👨‍🍳 **COOK'S TIP**

Make sure that the mixture fills the whole width of your skillet to enable the layers to remain intact.

This is a vegetarian version of chicken Kiev—the bean patties are topped with garlic and herb butter and coated in bread crumbs.

Kidney Bean Kiev

1 To make the garlic butter, put the butter, garlic, and parsley in a bowl and blend together with a wooden spoon. Place the garlic butter on to a sheet of baking parchment, roll into a cigar shape and wrap in the baking parchment. Chill in the refrigerator until required.

2 Using a potato masher, mash the red kidney beans in a mixing bowl and stir in ¾ cup of the bread crumbs until thoroughly blended.

3 Melt the butter in a heavy-based skillet. Add the leek and celery and sauté over a low heat, stirring constantly, for 3–4 minutes.

4 Add the bean mixture to the pan, together with the parsley, season with salt and pepper to taste and mix thoroughly. Remove the pan from the heat and set aside to cool slightly.

5 Divide the kidney bean mixture into 4 equal portions and shape them into ovals.

6 Slice the garlic butter into 4 pieces and place a slice in the center of each bean patty. With your hands, mold the bean mixture around the garlic butter to encase it completely.

7 Dip each bean patty into the beaten egg to coat and then roll in the remaining bread crumbs.

8 Heat a little oil in a skillet and cook the patties, turning once, for 7–10 minutes or until golden brown. Serve immediately.

SERVES 4

garlic butter
7 tbsp butter
3 garlic cloves, crushed
1 tbsp chopped fresh parsley

bean patties
3 cups canned red kidney beans
1¼ cups fresh white bread crumbs
2 tbsp butter
1 leek, chopped
1 celery stalk, chopped
1 tbsp chopped fresh parsley
1 egg, beaten
salt and pepper
vegetable oil, for shallow frying

NUTRITION
Calories *688*; Sugars *8 g*; Protein *17 g*; Carbohydrate *49 g*; Fat *49 g*; Saturates *20 g*

★★★ moderate

25 mins

20 mins

Bubble and squeak is best known as sautéed mashed potato and leftover greens served as an accompaniment.

Bubble *and* Squeak

SERVES 4

2²⁄₃ cups diced mealy potatoes
1½ cups Savoy cabbage, shredded
5 tbsp vegetable oil
2 leeks, chopped
1 garlic clove, crushed
8 oz/225 g smoked bean curd, cubed
salt and pepper
shredded cooked leek, to garnish

1 Cook the diced potatoes in a pan of lightly salted boiling water for 10 minutes, until tender. Drain and mash the potatoes.

2 Meanwhile, in a separate pan, blanch the cabbage in boiling water for 5 minutes. Drain well and add to the potato.

3 Heat the oil in a heavy-based skillet. Add the leeks and garlic and cook gently for 2–3 minutes. Stir into the potato and cabbage mixture.

4 Add the smoked bean curd and season well with salt and pepper. Cook over a medium heat for 10 minutes.

5 Carefully turn the whole mixture over and continue to cook over medium heat for another 5–7 minutes, or until crispy underneath.

6 Serve immediately, garnished with shredded leek.

NUTRITION
Calories *301*; Sugars *5 g*; Protein *11 g*;
Carbohydrate *24 g*; Fat *18 g*; Saturates *2 g*

easy

15 mins

40 mins

🍴 **COOK'S TIP**

This vegetarian version is a perfect entrée, as the smoked bean curd cubes added to the basic bubble and squeak make it very substantial and nourishing.

The freshness of lightly cooked summer vegetables is enhanced by the aromatic flavor of a tarragon and white wine dressing.

Sauté *of* Summer Vegetables

1 Cut the carrots in half lengthwise, slice the pole beans and zucchini, and halve the scallions and radishes, so that all the vegetables are cut to even-size pieces.

2 Melt the butter in a large, heavy skillet or wok. Add all the vegetables and cook them over medium heat, stirring frequently, until they are tender, but still crisp and firm to the bite.

3 Meanwhile, pour the olive oil, vinegar, and white wine into a small pan and add the sugar. Place over a low heat, stirring until the sugar has dissolved. Remove the pan from the heat and then add the chopped tarragon.

4 When the vegetables are just cooked, pour over the "dressing." Stir through, tossing the vegetables well to coat. Season to taste with salt and pepper and then transfer to a warmed serving dish.

5 Garnish with fresh tarragon sprigs and serve the sauté immediately.

SERVES 4

8 oz/225 g baby carrots, scrubbed
1 cup pole beans
2 zucchini, trimmed
1 bunch of large scallions
1 bunch of radishes
4 tbsp butter
2 tbsp light olive oil
2 tbsp white wine vinegar
4 tbsp dry white wine
1 tsp superfine sugar
1 tbsp chopped fresh tarragon
salt and pepper
fresh tarragon sprigs, to garnish

NUTRITION
Calories 217; Sugars 8 g; Protein 2 g;
Carbohydrate 9 g; Fat 18 g; Saturates 9 g

⊛ very easy

◷ 10 mins

◷ 10–15 mins

This vegetarian version of paella is packed with vegetables and nuts for a truly delicious and simple dish.

Cashew Nut Paella

SERVES 4

2 tbsp olive oil
1 tbsp butter
1 red onion, chopped
²/₃ cup risotto rice
1 tsp ground turmeric
1 tsp ground cumin
½ tsp chili powder
3 garlic cloves, crushed
1 fresh green chile, seeded and sliced
1 green bell pepper, halved, seeded, and diced
1 red bell pepper, halved, seeded, and diced
¾ cup baby corn ears, halved lengthwise
2 tbsp pitted black olives
1 large tomato, seeded and diced
2 cups Fresh Vegetable Bouillon (see page 16)
¾ cup unsalted cashew nuts
½ cup frozen peas
2 tbsp chopped fresh parsley
pinch of cayenne pepper
salt and pepper
fresh herbs, to garnish

NUTRITION

Calories *406*; Sugars *8 g*; Protein *10 g*; Carbohydrate *44 g*; Fat *22 g*; Saturates *6 g*

easy

15 mins

35 mins

1 Heat the olive oil and butter in a large skillet or paella pan until the butter has melted.

2 Add the onion and cook over a medium heat, stirring constantly, for about 2–3 minutes until soft.

3 Stir in the rice, turmeric, cumin, chili powder, garlic, sliced chile, green and red bell peppers, corn ears, olives, and tomato and cook over medium heat, stirring occasionally, for 1–2 minutes.

4 Pour in the bouillon and bring the mixture to a boil. Reduce the heat and cook gently, stirring constantly, for 20 minutes.

5 Add the cashew nuts and peas and cook, stirring occasionally, for a further 5 minutes. Season to taste and sprinkle with parsley and cayenne pepper.

6 Transfer the paella to warm serving plates, garnish with fresh herbs, and serve immediately.

East meets West in this delicious dish. Prepare all the vegetables and cook the pasta in advance, then the dish can be cooked in a few minutes.

Vegetable Pasta Stir-fry

1 Cook the pasta in a large pan of boiling, lightly salted water, adding the tablespoon of olive oil. When tender, but still firm to the bite, drain the pasta, return to the pan, cover, and keep warm.

2 Cook the carrots and baby corn ears in boiling, salted water for 2 minutes. Drain, plunge into cold water to prevent further cooking, and drain again.

3 Heat the peanut oil in a large skillet over a medium heat. Add the gingerroot and stir-fry for 1 minute, to flavor the oil. Remove the gingerroot with a draining spoon and discard.

4 Add the onion, garlic, celery, and bell peppers to the oil and stir-fry over medium heat for 2 minutes. Add the carrots and baby corn ears, and stir-fry for a further 2 minutes, then stir in the reserved pasta.

5 Put the cornstarch in a small bowl and mix to a smooth paste with the water. Stir in the soy sauce, the sherry, and the honey.

6 Pour the sauce into the pan with the pasta, stir well, and cook for 2 minutes, stirring once or twice. Taste the sauce and season with hot pepper sauce if wished. Serve with a steamed green vegetable, such as snow peas.

SERVES 4

4 cups dried whole-wheat penne pasta
1 tbsp olive oil
2 carrots, thinly sliced
10 –12 baby corn ears
3 tbsp peanut oil
1-inch/2.5-cm piece fresh gingerroot, sliced
1 large onion, sliced thinly
1 garlic clove, sliced thinly
3 celery stalks, sliced thinly
1 small red bell pepper, halved, seeded, and sliced into matchstick strips
1 small green bell pepper, halved, seeded, and sliced into matchstick strips
salt
steamed snow peas, to serve

sauce
1 tsp cornstarch
2 tbsp water
3 tbsp soy sauce
3 tbsp dry sherry
1 tsp clear honey
dash of hot pepper sauce (optional)

NUTRITION
Calories *383*; Sugars *18 g*; Protein *14 g*;
Carbohydrate *32 g*; Fat *23 g*; Saturates *8 g*

easy

20 mins

25 mins

Serve this dish with plain noodles or fluffy white rice for a filling and flavorful Asian meal.

Sweet *and* Sour Vegetables

SERVES 4

1 tbsp peanut oil
2 garlic cloves, crushed
1 tsp grated fresh gingerroot
6–8 baby corn ears
¾ cup snow peas
1 carrot, cut into matchsticks
1 green bell pepper, halved, seeded, and cut into matchsticks
8 scallions
2 oz/55 g canned bamboo shoots
8 oz/225 g marinated firm bean curd, cubed
2 tbsp dry sherry or Chinese rice wine
2 tbsp rice wine vinegar
2 tbsp clear honey
1 tbsp light soy sauce
⅔ cup Fresh Vegetable Bouillon (see page 16)
1 tbsp cornstarch
noodles or boiled rice, to serve

1 Heat the oil in a preheated wok until it is almost smoking. Add the garlic and the grated fresh gingerroot and cook over medium heat, stirring frequently, for 30 seconds.

2 Add the baby corn ears, the snow peas, and the carrot and pepper matchsticks, and stir-fry for about 5 minutes, or until the vegetables are tender, but still crisp.

3 Add the scallions, bamboo shoots, and bean curd and cook for 2 minutes.

4 Stir in the sherry or Chinese rice wine, the rice wine vinegar, honey, soy sauce, vegetable bouillon, and cornstarch and bring to a boil. Reduce the heat to low and simmer for 2 minutes, until heated through.

5 Transfer to warmed serving dishes and serve immediately.

NUTRITION
Calories *401*; Sugars *16 g*; Protein *14 g*;
Carbohydrate *70 g*; Fat *9 g*; Saturates *2 g*

⭐ very easy
🕐 10 mins
🕐 15 mins

Grated carrots, zucchini, and feta cheese are combined with cumin seeds, poppy seeds, curry powder, and chopped fresh parsley.

Feta Cheese Patties

1 Grate the carrots, zucchini, onion, and feta cheese coarsely, either by hand or process in a food processor.

2 Combine the flour, cumin seeds, poppy seeds, curry powder, and parsley in a large bowl. Season with salt and pepper.

3 Add the carrot and zucchini mixture to the seasoned flour, tossing well to combine. Stir in the beaten egg.

4 Heat the butter and vegetable oil in a large, heavy skillet. Place heaped tablespoonfuls of the patty mixture in the skillet, flattening them slightly with the back of the spoon. Cook over low heat, for about 2 minutes on each side, until crisp and golden brown. Drain on paper towels and keep warm. Cook more patties in the same way until all the mixture is used.

5 Serve immediately, garnished with fresh herb sprigs.

SERVES 4

2 large carrots
1 large zucchini
1 small onion
2 oz /55 g feta cheese
4 tbsp all-purpose flour
$\frac{1}{4}$ tsp cumin seeds
$\frac{1}{2}$ tsp poppy seeds
1 tsp medium curry powder
1 tbsp chopped fresh parsley
1 egg, beaten
2 tbsp butter
2 tbsp vegetable oil
salt and pepper
fresh herb sprigs, to garnish

NUTRITION
Calories 217; Sugars 6 g; Protein 6 g;
Carbohydrate 12 g; Fat 16 g; Saturates 7 g

⭐⭐ easy

 15 mins

15 mins

20 mins

Casseroles *and* Bakes

Anyone who ever thought that vegetarian meals were dull will be proved wrong by the rich variety of dishes in this chapter. You'll recognize influences from Mexican and Chinese cooking, but there are also traditional stews and casseroles, as well as hearty bakes and roasts. They all make exciting meals, at any time of year, and for virtually any occasion. Don't be afraid to substitute your own personal favorite ingredients where appropriate. There is no reason why you cannot enjoy experimenting and adding your own touch to these imaginative ideas.

This is a really hearty dish, perfect for cold days when a filling hot meal is just what you need to keep the winter out.

Lentil *and* Rice Casserole

SERVES 4

1 cup split red lentils, washed
generous ¼ cup long grain rice
5 cups Fresh Vegetable Bouillon
   (see page 16)
1 leek, cut into chunks
3 garlic cloves, crushed
2 cans canned chopped tomatoes
1 tsp ground cumin
1 tsp chili powder
1 tsp garam masala
1 red bell pepper, halved, deseeded
   and sliced
1 cup small broccoli flowerets
8 baby corn ears, halved lengthwise
⅔ cup green beans, halved
1 tbsp shredded fresh basil
salt and pepper
fresh basil sprigs, to garnish

1 Place the lentils, rice, and vegetable stock in a large flameproof casserole and cook over low heat, stirring occasionally, for 20 minutes.

2 Add the leek, garlic, tomatoes, ground cumin, chili powder, garam masala, sliced bell pepper, broccoli, corn ears, and green beans to the casserole.

3 Bring the mixture to a boil, reduce the heat, cover, and simmer for a further 10–15 minutes or until all the vegetables are tender.

4 Add the shredded basil and season with salt and pepper to taste.

5 Garnish with fresh basil sprigs and serve immediately.

NUTRITION
Calories *312*; Sugars *9 g*; Protein *20 g*;
Carbohydrate *51 g*; Fat *2 g*; Saturates *0.4 g*

easy

15 mins

20 mins

COOK'S TIP

You can vary the rice in this recipe—use brown or wild rice, if you prefer.

Seasonal fresh vegetables are casseroled with lentils, then topped with a ring of fresh cheese biscuits to make this tasty pot pie.

Winter Vegetable Cobbler

1 Heat the oil and cook the garlic and onions for 5 minutes. Add the celery, rutabaga, carrots, and cauliflower and cook for 2–3 minutes. Add the mushrooms, tomatoes, and lentils. Mix the cornstarch and water and stir into the pan with the bouillon, Tabasco, and oregano.

2 Transfer to a casserole, cover, and bake in a preheated oven, 350°F/ 180°C, for 20 minutes.

3 To make the topping, sift the flour with a pinch of salt into a bowl. Rub in the butter, then stir in most of the cheese and the herbs. Beat the egg with the milk and add enough to the dry ingredients to make a soft dough. Knead lightly, roll out to ½-inch/1-cm thick and cut into 2-inch/5-cm rounds.

4 Remove the casserole from the oven and increase the temperature to 400°F/200°C. Arrange the biscuits around the edge of the casserole, brush with the remaining egg and milk, and sprinkle with the reserved cheese. Cook for a further 10–12 minutes. Garnish and serve.

SERVES 4

1 tbsp olive oil
1 garlic clove, crushed
8 small onions, halved
2 celery stalks, sliced
1¼ cups chopped, rutabaga
2 carrots, sliced
½ small cauliflower, broken into flowerets
3¼ cups sliced mushrooms
2 cups canned chopped tomatoes
¼ cup red lentils, washed
2 tbsp cornstarch and 3–4 tbsp water
1¼ cups Fresh Vegetable Bouillon (see page 16)
2 tsp Tabasco sauce
2 tsp chopped fresh oregano

biscuit topping
2 cups self-rising flour
4 tbsp butter
1 cup grated sharp colby cheese
2 tsp chopped fresh oregano
1 egg, lightly beaten
⅔ cup milk
salt

NUTRITION
Calories *734*; Sugars *22 g*; Protein *27 g*;
Carbohydrate *96 g*; Fat *30 g*; Saturates *16 g*

⭐⭐⭐   moderate

🕐   20 mins

🕐   40 mins

The perfect dish to serve for Sunday lunch. Roast vegetables make a succulent accompaniment.

Lentil Roast

SERVES 4

1¼ cups red lentils, washed
2 cups Fresh Vegetable Bouillon
  (see page 16)
1 bay leaf
1 tbsp butter or margarine, softened
2 tbsp dried whole-wheat bread crumbs
2 cups grated sharp colby cheese
1 leek, chopped finely
2 cups white mushrooms, chopped finely
1½ cups fresh whole-wheat bread crumbs
2 tbsp chopped parsley
1 tbsp lemon juice
2 eggs, lightly beaten
salt and pepper
flatleaf parsley sprigs, to garnish
mixed roasted vegetables, to serve

1 Put the lentils, bouillon, and bay leaf in a pan. Bring to a boil, cover, and simmer gently for 15–20 minutes, until all the liquid is absorbed and the lentils have softened. Discard the bay leaf.

2 Line the base of a 2-lb/900-g loaf pan with baking parchment. Grease with the butter or margarine and sprinkle with the dried bread crumbs.

3 Stir the grated cheese, chopped leek and mushrooms, bread crumbs, and parsley into the lentils.

4 Bind the mixture together with the lemon juice and eggs. Season with salt and pepper. Spoon into the prepared loaf pan and smooth the top.

5 Bake in a preheated oven, 375°F/190°C, for about 1 hour, until golden.

6 Loosen the loaf with a spatula and turn on to a warmed serving plate.

7 Garnish with parsley and serve sliced, with roasted vegetables.

NUTRITION

Calories 400; Sugars 2 g; Protein 26 g;
Carbohydrate 32 g; Fat 20 g; Saturates 10 g

✪✪✪✪ challenging

15 mins

1 hr 20 mins

Toasted almonds are combined with sesame seeds, rice, and vegetables in this tasty roast. Serve it with a delicious onion and mushroom sauce.

Almond *and* Sesame Roast

1 Heat the oil in a large skillet and cook the onion gently for 2–3 minutes. Add the rice and cook gently for 5–6 minutes, stirring frequently.

2 Add the bouillon, bring to a boil, lower the heat, and simmer for 15 minutes or until the rice is tender. Add a little extra water if necessary. Remove from the heat and transfer to a large mixing bowl.

3 Add the carrot, leek, sesame seeds, chopped almonds, ground almonds, cheese, beaten eggs, and herbs. Mix well and season with salt and pepper to taste. Transfer the mixture to a greased 1-lb/450-g loaf pan, smoothing the surface. Bake in a preheated oven, 350°F/180°C, for 1 hour until set and firm. Let stand in the pan for 10 minutes.

4 To make the sauce, melt the butter in a small pan and cook the onion until dark golden brown. Add the mushrooms and cook for 2 minutes. Stir in the flour, cook gently for 1 minute, then gradually add the bouillon. Bring to a boil, stirring constantly, until thickened and blended. Season to taste with salt and pepper.

5 Turn out the nut roast, slice, and serve, garnished with parsley sprigs, with fresh vegetables, accompanied by the onion and mushroom sauce.

SERVES 4

2 tbsp sesame or olive oil
1 small onion, finely chopped
$\frac{1}{2}$ cup risotto rice
$1\frac{1}{4}$ cups Fresh Vegetable Bouillon (see page 16)
1 large carrot, grated
1 large leek, chopped finely
2 tsp sesame seeds, toasted
$\frac{3}{4}$ cup chopped almonds, toasted
$\frac{1}{2}$ cup ground almonds
$\frac{3}{4}$ cup grated sharp colby cheese
2 eggs, beaten
1 tsp mixed dried herbs
butter, for greasing
salt and pepper
fresh flatleaf parsley sprigs, to garnish
fresh vegetables, to serve

sauce
2 tbsp butter
1 small onion, chopped finely
$1\frac{1}{2}$ cups finely chopped mushrooms
4 tbsp all-purpose flour
$1\frac{1}{4}$ cups Fresh Vegetable Bouillon

NUTRITION
Calories *612*; Sugars *7 g*; Protein *22 g*;
Carbohydrate *29 g*; Fat *46 g*; Saturates *13 g*

⭐⭐⭐   moderate
🕐   20–30 mins
🕐   1 hr 30 mins

A wonderful mixture of red lentils, bean curd, and vegetables is cooked beneath a crunchy potato topping for a really hearty meal.

Potato-Topped Lentil Bake

SERVES 4

topping
4¹/₂ cups diced mealy potatoes
2 tbsp butter
1 tbsp milk
¹/₂ cup chopped pecan nuts
2 tbsp chopped fresh thyme
thyme sprigs, to garnish

filling
1¹/₄ cups red lentils, washed
¹/₄ cup butter
1 leek, sliced
2 garlic cloves, crushed
1 celery stalk, chopped
1¹/₄ cups broccoli flowerets
6 oz/175 g smoked bean curd, cubed
2 tsp tomato paste
salt and pepper

NUTRITION
Calories *627*; Sugars *7 g*; Protein *26 g*;
Carbohydrate *66 g*; Fat *30 g*; Saturates *13 g*

⊛⊛⊛ moderate
🕐 10 mins
🕐 1 hr 30 mins

1 To make the topping, cook the diced potatoes in a pan of boiling water for 10–15 minutes, or until cooked through. Drain well, add the butter and milk, and mash thoroughly. Stir in the chopped pecan nuts and the chopped thyme and set aside.

2 Cook the lentils in boiling water for 20–30 minutes, or until tender. Drain and set aside.

3 Melt the butter in a skillet. Add the leek, garlic, celery, and broccoli. Fry over medium heat, stirring frequently, for 5 minutes, until soft.

4 Add the bean curd cubes. Stir in the lentils, together with the tomato paste. Season with salt and pepper to taste, then turn the mixture into the base of a shallow ovenproof dish.

5 Spoon the mashed potato on top of the lentil mixture, spreading to cover it completely.

6 Cook the lentil bake in a preheated oven, 400°F/200°C, for about 30–35 minutes, or until the topping is golden brown. Remove the bake from the oven, garnish with sprigs of fresh thyme, and serve hot.

🍳 **COOK'S TIP**

You can use almost any combination of your favorite vegetables in this dish.

This bake of corn and kidney beans, flavored with chile and fresh cilantro, is topped with crispy cheese cornbread.

Mexican Chile Corn Pie

1 Heat the oil in a large skillet and gently panfry the garlic, bell peppers, and celery for 5–6 minutes until just softened.

2 Stir in the chili powder, tomatoes, corn, beans, and seasoning. Bring to a boil and simmer for 10 minutes. Stir in the cilantro and spoon into an ovenproof dish.

3 To make the topping, mix together the cornmeal, flour, salt, and baking powder. Make a well in the center, add the egg, milk, and oil and beat until a smooth batter is formed.

4 Spoon over the bell pepper and corn mixture and sprinkle with the cheese. Bake in a preheated oven, at 425°C/220°F, for 25–30 minutes until golden and firm.

5 Garnish with cilantro sprigs and serve immediately with a tomato and avocado salad.

SERVES 4

1 tbsp corn oil
2 garlic cloves, crushed
1 red bell pepper, halved, seeded, and diced
1 green bell pepper, halved and diced
1 celery stalk, diced
1 tsp hot chili powder
2 cups canned chopped tomatoes
11¹/₂ oz/325 g canned corn, drained
1 cup kidney beans, drained and rinsed
2 tbsp chopped fresh cilantro, and sprigs, to garnish
salt and pepper
tomato and avocado salad, to serve

topping
²/₃ cup cornmeal
1 tbsp all-purpose flour
¹/₂ tsp salt
2 tsp baking powder
1 egg, beaten
6 tbsp milk
1 tbsp corn oil
1 cup grated sharp colby cheese

NUTRITION
Calories *519*; Sugars *17 g*; Protein *22 g*; Carbohydrate *61 g*; Fat *22 g*; Saturates *9 g*

⚫⚫⚫ moderate

🕐 25 mins

🕐 45 mins

In this recipe, a variety of vegetables are cooked under a layer of potatoes, topped with cheese, and cooked until golden brown.

Vegetable Hotpot

SERVES 4

8 oz/675 g potatoes, sliced thinly
2 tbsp vegetable oil
1 red onion, halved and sliced
1 leek, sliced
2 garlic cloves, crushed
1 carrot, cut into chunks
1 cup broccoli flowerets
scant cup cauliflower flowerets
2 small turnips, cut into fourths
¼ cup all-purpose flour
3 cups Fresh Vegetable Bouillon
   (see page 16)
⅔ cup hard cider
1 eating apple, cored and sliced
2 tbsp chopped fresh sage
pinch of cayenne pepper
½ cup grated colby cheese
salt and pepper

1 Cook the potato slices in a pan of boiling water for 10 minutes. Drain thoroughly and reserve.

2 Heat the vegetable oil in a flameproof casserole. Add the onion, leek, and garlic to the oil and sauté, stirring occasionally, for 2–3 minutes.

3 Add the remaining vegetables and cook, stirring constantly, for a further 3–4 minutes.

4 Stir in the flour and cook for 1 minute. Gradually add the bouillon and cider and bring to a boil. Add the apple, sage, and cayenne pepper and season.

5 Remove from the heat and transfer the vegetables to an ovenproof dish.

6 Arrange the potato slices on top of the vegetable mixture to cover.

7 Sprinkle the grated cheese on top of the potato slices and cook in a preheated oven, 375°F/190°C, for about 30–35 minutes or until the potato is golden brown and beginning to go crisp around the edges. Serve the vegetable hotpot immediately, straight from the dish.

NUTRITION
Calories 279; Sugars 12 g; Protein 10 g;
Carbohydrate 34 g; Fat 11 g; Saturates 4 g

easy

25 mins

1 hr

A tasty, simple supper dish of choux pastry and crisp green vegetables. The choux pastry ring can be filled with all kinds of vegetables.

Green Vegetable Gougère

1 Strain the flour on to a piece of baking parchment. Cut the butter into dice and put in a pan with the water. Heat until the butter has melted.

2 Do not let the water boil, and tip in the flour all at once. Beat until the mixture becomes thick. Remove from the heat and continue to beat until the mixture is glossy and comes away from the sides of the pan.

3 Transfer to a mixing bowl and cool for 10 minutes. Gradually beat in the eggs, a little at a time, making sure they are thoroughly incorporated after each addition. Stir in ½ cup of the cheese and season with salt and pepper.

4 Place spoonfuls of the mixture in a 9-inch/23-cm circle on a dampened cookie sheet. Brush with milk and sprinkle with the remaining cheese.

5 Bake in a preheated oven, 425°F/ 220°C, for 30–35 minutes, until golden and crisp. Transfer to a warmed serving plate.

6 Meanwhile, make the filling. Heat the butter or margarine and the olive oil in a large skillet and stir-fry the leeks and cabbage for 2 minutes. Add the beansprouts, lime peel, and juice and stir-fry for 1 minute. Season to taste.

7 Pile into the center of the pastry ring. Garnish with lime slices and serve.

SERVES 4

1 cup all-purpose flour
½ cup plus 1 tbsp butter
1¼ cups water
4 eggs, beaten
¾ cup grated Swiss cheese
1 tbsp milk
salt and pepper

filling

2 tbsp garlic and herb butter or margarine
2 tsp olive oil
2 leeks, shredded
2 cups green cabbage, shredded finely
1½ cups beansprouts
½ tsp grated lime peel
1 tbsp lime juice
celery salt and pepper
lime slices, to garnish

NUTRITION
Calories *672*; Sugars *6 g*; Protein *19 g*; Carbohydrate *36 g*; Fat *51 g*; Saturates *14 g*

⭐⭐⭐ moderate
🕐 30 mins
🕐 40 mins

These strudels look really impressive and are perfect if friends are coming round or for a more formal dinner party dish.

Vegetable *and* Bean Curd Strudels

SERVES 4

filling
2 tbsp vegetable oil
2 tbsp butter
¾ cup finely diced potatoes
1 leek, shredded
2 garlic cloves, crushed
1 tsp garam masala
½ tsp chili powder
½ tsp turmeric
¼ cup okra, sliced
1½ cups sliced white mushrooms
2 tomatoes, diced
8 oz/225 g firm bean curd, diced
salt and pepper

pastry
12 oz/350 g phyllo pastry
2 tbsp butter, melted

1 To make the filling, heat the vegetable oil and butter in a skillet. Add the potatoes and leek to the skillet and cook, stirring constantly, for 2–3 minutes. Add the garlic and spices, okra, mushrooms, tomatoes, and bean curd, and season to taste with salt and pepper. Cook, stirring, for 5–7 minutes, or until the mixture is tender.

2 Lay the pastry out on a cutting board and brush each individual sheet with melted butter. Place 3 sheets on top of one another; repeat to make 4 stacks.

3 Spoon a quarter of the filling along the center of each stack and brush the edges with melted butter. Fold the short edges in and roll up lengthwise to form a cigar shape. Brush the outside with melted butter. Place the strudels on a greased cookie sheet.

4 Cook in a preheated oven, 375°F/190°C, for 20 minutes, or until the strudels are golden brown and crisp. Transfer them to a warm serving dish and serve immediately.

NUTRITION
Calories *485*; Sugars *5 g*; Protein *16 g*;
Carbohydrate *47 g*; Fat *27 g*; Saturates *5 g*

⭐⭐⭐ moderate
🕐 25 mins
🕐 30 mins

These puffs, filled with garlic, mushrooms, and spinach, are easy to make and bake to an appealing golden brown.

Mushroom *and* Spinach Puffs

1 Melt the butter in a skillet. Add the onion and garlic and sauté over low heat, stirring, for 3–4 minutes, until the onion has softened.

2 Add the mushrooms, spinach, and nutmeg and cook them over medium heat, stirring occasionally, for 2–3 minutes.

3 Stir in the heavy cream, mixing thoroughly. Season with salt and pepper to taste and remove the pan from the heat. Let the mixture stand.

4 Roll out the pastry on a lightly floured counter and cut it into 4 6-inch/15-cm rounds, using a bowl or a saucer as a guide.

5 Dampen the pastry edges. Put a quarter of the filling onto 1 half of each round and fold the pastry over to encase it. Press down to seal the edges and brush with the beaten egg. Sprinkle with the poppy seeds.

6 Place the puffs on a dampened cookie sheet and cook in a preheated oven, 400°F/200°C, for 20 minutes, until the pastry is risen and golden brown in color. Serve immediately.

SERVES 4

2 tbsp butter
1 red onion, halved and sliced
2 garlic cloves, crushed
3 cups sliced open-cap mushrooms
3 tightly packed cups young spinach
pinch of nutmeg
4 tbsp heavy cream
8 oz/225 g ready-made puff pie dough, thawed if frozen
flour, for dusting
1 egg, beaten
salt and pepper
2 tsp poppy seeds

NUTRITION
Calories *467*; Sugars *4 g*; Protein *8 g*; Carbohydrate *24 g*; Fat *38 g*; Saturates *18 g*

⭐⭐⭐   moderate

🕒   20 mins

🕐   30 mins

This mouthwateringly attractive tart is full of Mediterranean flavors— spinach, red bell peppers, ricotta cheese, and pine nuts.

Italian Vegetable Tart

SERVES 4

½ lb/225 g frozen phyllo pastry, thawed
½ cup butter, melted
12 oz/350 g frozen spinach, thawed
2 eggs
⅔ cup light cream
1 cup ricotta cheese
1 red bell pepper, halved, deseeded, and
  sliced into strips
½ cup pine nuts
salt and pepper

1 Use the sheets of phyllo pastry to line an 8 inch/20 cm quiche pan, brushing each layer with melted butter.

2 Put the spinach into a strainer and squeeze out the excess moisture with the back of a spoon or your hand. Form the spinach into 8–9 small balls and arrange them in the prepared quiche pan.

3 Beat the eggs, cream, and ricotta cheese together until thoroughly blended. Season to taste with salt and pepper and pour over the spinach.

4 Put the remaining butter into a pan. Add the red bell pepper strips and sauté over low heat, stirring frequently, for about 4–5 minutes, until soft. Arrange the strips on the tart.

5 Scatter the pine nuts over the surface and bake in a preheated oven, 375°F/190°C, for about 20–25 minutes, until the filling has set and the pastry is golden brown. Serve the tart immediately or let cool completely and serve at room temperature.

NUTRITION

Calories *488*; Sugars *7 g*; Protein *13 g*;
Carbohydrate *21 g*; Fat *40 g*; Saturates *19 g*

moderate

30 mins

30 mins

COOK'S TIP

If you are not fond of bell peppers, you could use mushrooms instead. Exotic mushrooms would be especially delicious. Add a few sliced sun-dried tomatoes for extra color and flavor.

Different varieties of mushrooms are becoming more widely available in food stores, so use this recipe to make the most of them.

Mushroom Tarts

1 Cut the sheets of phyllo pastry into 4-inch/10-cm squares and line 4 individual tart pans, brushing each layer with melted butter. Line the pastry with baking parchment and baking beans. Bake in a preheated oven, 400°F/200°C, for 6–8 minutes until golden.

2 Remove the tarts from the oven and carefully take out the baking parchment and baking beans. Reduce the oven temperature to 350°F/180°C.

3 Put any remaining butter into a large pan with the hazelnut oil and cook the pine nuts until golden brown. Remove the nuts from the pan and drain on paper towels.

4 Add the mushrooms to the pan and cook gently, stirring frequently, for about 4–5 minutes. Add the parsley and season to taste .

5 Spoon one-quarter of the goat cheese into the base of each cooked phyllo tart. Divide the mushrooms equally among them and sprinkle the pine nuts evenly over the top.

6 Return the tarts to the oven for about 5 minutes to heat through.

7 Garnish the tarts with parsley sprigs. Serve with lettuce, tomatoes, cucumber, and scallions.

SERVES 4

1 lb/450 g phyllo pastry, thawed if frozen
½ cup butter, melted
1 tbsp hazelnut oil
4 tbsp pine nuts
12 oz/350 g mixed mushrooms, such as white, crimini, oyster, and shiitake
2 tsp chopped fresh parsley
½ lb/225 g soft goat cheese
salt and pepper
fresh parsley sprigs to garnish

to serve
lettuce
tomatoes
cucumber
scallions

NUTRITION
Calories *494*; Sugars *2 g*; Protein *9 g*; Carbohydrate *38 g*; Fat *35 g*; Saturates *18 g*

⭐⭐⭐   moderate

🕐   15 mins

🕐   20 mins

This is a savory version of a cheesecake with a layer of fried potatoes as a delicious base. Use frozen mixed vegetables for the topping, if desired.

Vegetable Cake

S E R V E S   4

base
2 tbsp vegetable oil, plus extra for brushing
2 lb 12 oz/1.25 kg waxy potatoes, sliced

topping
1 tbsp vegetable oil
1 leek, chopped
1 zucchini, grated
1 red bell pepper, halved, seeded, and diced
1 green bell pepper, halved, seeded, and diced
1 carrot, grated
2 tsp chopped fresh parsley
1 cup full-fat soft cheese
4 tbsp grated sharp colby cheese
2 eggs, beaten
salt and pepper
shredded cooked leek, to garnish
salad, to serve

N U T R I T I O N
Calories *502*; Sugars *8 g*; Protein *16 g*;
Carbohydrate *41 g*; Fat *31 g*; Saturates *14 g*

⭐⭐   easy
🕐   20 mins
🕐   45 mins

1 Brush an 8-inch/20-cm springform cake pan with oil.

2 To make the base, heat the oil in a skillet. Cook the potato slices until softened and browned. Drain on paper towels and place in the bottom of the prepared pan.

3 To make the topping, heat the oil in a separate skillet. Add the leek and cook over a low heat, stirring frequently, for 3–4 minutes until softened.

4 Add the zucchini, bell peppers, carrot, and parsley to the skillet and cook over a low heat for 5–7 minutes or until the vegetables have softened.

5 Meanwhile, beat the cheeses and eggs together in a bowl. Stir in the vegetables and season to taste with salt and pepper. Spoon the cake mixture evenly over the potato base.

6 Cook in a preheated oven, 375°F/190°C, for 20–25 minutes, until the cake is set.

7 Remove the vegetable cake from the pan, transfer to a warm serving plate, garnish with shredded leek, and serve with a crisp salad.

Hot soufflés look very impressive if served as soon as they come out of the oven, otherwise they will sink quite quickly.

Leek *and* Herb Soufflé

SERVES 4

1 tbsp olive oil
12 oz/350 g baby leeks, chopped finely
½ cup Fresh Vegetable Bouillon (see page 16)
½ cup walnuts
2 eggs, separated
2 tbsp chopped mixed fresh herbs
2 tbsp plain yogurt
salt and pepper

1 Heat the oil in a skillet. Add the leeks and sauté over medium heat, stirring occasionally, for 2–3 minutes.

2 Add the vegetable bouillon to the skillet, lower the heat, and simmer gently for a further 5 minutes.

3 Place the walnuts in a food processor and process until chopped finely. Add the leek mixture to the nuts and process briefly to form a purée. Transfer to a mixing bowl.

4 Mix together the egg yolks, the herbs, and the yogurt until thoroughly combined. Pour the egg mixture into the leek purée. Season with salt and pepper to taste and mix well.

5 In a separate, grease-free mixing bowl, whisk the egg whites until firm peaks form.

6 Fold the egg whites into the leek mixture. Spoon the mixture into a lightly greased 3½ cup/880 ml soufflé dish and place on a warmed cookie sheet.

7 Cook the soufflé in a preheated oven, 350°F/180°C, for 35–40 minutes, or until well risen, set, and golden brown on top. Serve immediately.

NUTRITION
Calories *182*; Sugars *4 g*; Protein *8 g*;
Carbohydrate *5 g*; Fat *15 g*; Saturates *2 g*

moderate

15 mins

45-50 mins

This is a quick dish to prepare and it can be left to cook in the oven without needing any more attention.

Cheese *and* Potato Layer Bake

SERVES 4

2 lb/900 g unpeeled waxy potatoes,
  cut into wedges
2 tbsp butter
1 red onion, halved and sliced
2 garlic cloves, crushed
¼ cup all-purpose flour
2½ cups milk
14 oz/400 g canned artichoke hearts in
  brine, drained, and halved
1 generous cup frozen mixed
  vegetables, thawed
1¼ cups grated Swiss cheese
1¼ cups grated sharp colby cheese
½ cup crumbled Gorgonzola
⅓ cup freshly grated Parmesan cheese
8 oz/225 g bean curd, sliced
2 tbsp chopped fresh thyme
salt and pepper
fresh thyme sprigs, to garnish

1 Cook the potato wedges in a pan of boiling water for 10 minutes. Drain thoroughly.

2 Meanwhile, melt the butter in a pan. Add the sliced onion and garlic and cook over low heat, stirring frequently, for 2–3 minutes.

3 Stir the flour into the pan and cook for 1 minute. Gradually add the milk and bring to a boil, stirring constantly.

4 Reduce the heat. Add the artichoke hearts, mixed vegetables, half of each of the 4 cheeses, and the bean curd to the pan, mixing well. Stir in the thyme and season with salt and pepper to taste.

5 Arrange a layer of potato wedges in the base of a shallow ovenproof dish. Spoon the vegetable mixture over the top and cover with the remaining potato wedges. Sprinkle the remaining 4 cheeses on top.

6 Cook in a preheated oven, 400°F/200°C, for 30 minutes, or until the potatoes are cooked and the top is golden brown. Serve the bake garnished with fresh thyme sprigs.

NUTRITION
Calories 766; Sugars 14 g; Protein 44 g;
Carbohydrate 60 g; Fat 40 g; Saturates 23 g

easy

25 mins

45 mins

Fennel tastes fabulous in this creamy sauce, flavored with caraway seeds. A crunchy bread crumb topping gives an interesting texture.

Creamy Baked Fennel

1 Bring a pan of water to a boil and add the lemon juice and fennel. Cook for 2–3 minutes to blanch, drain well, and place in a greased casserole.

2 Beat the soft cheese in a bowl until smooth. Add the cream, milk, and beaten egg, and beat until combined. Season to taste with salt and pepper and pour the mixture over the fennel.

3 Melt 1 tablespoon of the butter in a small skillet and fry the caraway seeds over a low heat, stirring constantly, for 1–2 minutes until they release their aroma. Sprinkle them over the fennel.

4 Melt the remaining butter in a skillet. Add the bread crumbs and fry over low heat, stirring frequently, until lightly browned. Sprinkle them evenly over the top of the fennel.

5 Place in a preheated oven, 350°F/180°C, and bake for 25–30 minutes or until the fennel is tender. Serve immediately, garnished with parsley sprigs.

SERVES 4

2 tbsp lemon juice
2 fennel bulbs, sliced thinly
4 tbsp butter, plus extra for greasing
1/2 cup lowfat soft cheese
2/3 cup light cream
2/3 cup milk
1 egg, lightly beaten
2 tsp caraway seeds
1 cup fresh white bread crumbs
salt and pepper
fresh parsley sprigs, to garnish

NUTRITION
Calories 292; Sugars 5 g; Protein 10 g; Carbohydrate 12 g; Fat 23 g; Saturates 14 g

moderate

10 mins

35–40 mins

Similar to a simple moussaka, this recipe is made up of layers of eggplant, tomato, and potato baked with a yogurt topping.

Potato *and* Eggplant Gratin

SERVES 4

1 lb/450 g waxy potatoes, sliced
1 tbsp vegetable oil
1 onion, chopped
2 garlic cloves, crushed
1 lb/450 g bean curd, diced
2 tbsp tomato paste
$\frac{1}{2}$ cup all-purpose flour
1$\frac{1}{4}$ cups Fresh Vegetable Bouillon
 (see page 16)
2 large tomatoes, sliced
1 eggplant, sliced
2 tbsp chopped fresh thyme
scant 2 cups plain yogurt
2 eggs, beaten
salt and pepper
salad, to serve

NUTRITION

Calories *409*; Sugars *17 g*; Protein *28 g*;
Carbohydrate *45 g*; Fat *14 g*; Saturates *3 g*

moderate

25 mins

1 hr 15 mins

1 Cook the sliced potatoes in a pan of boiling water for 10 minutes, until tender, but not breaking up. Drain and then set aside.

2 Heat the oil in a skillet. Add the onion and garlic and cook, stirring occasionally, for 2–3 minutes.

3 Add the bean curd, tomato paste, and flour, and cook for 1 minute. Gradually stir in the bouillon and bring to a boil, stirring. Reduce the heat and simmer for 10 minutes.

4 Arrange a layer of the potato slices in the base of a deep ovenproof dish. Spoon the bean curd mixture evenly on top. Layer the sliced tomatoes, then the eggplant, and the remaining potato slices, on top of the bean curd mixture, making sure it is completely covered. Sprinkle with thyme.

5 Mix the yogurt and beaten eggs together in a bowl and season to taste with salt and pepper. Spoon the yogurt topping over the sliced potatoes to cover them completely.

6 Bake in a preheated oven, 375°F/ 190°C, for about 35–45 minutes or until the topping is browned. Serve with a crisp salad.

COOK'S TIP

You can use marinated or smoked bean curd for extra flavor, if you wish.

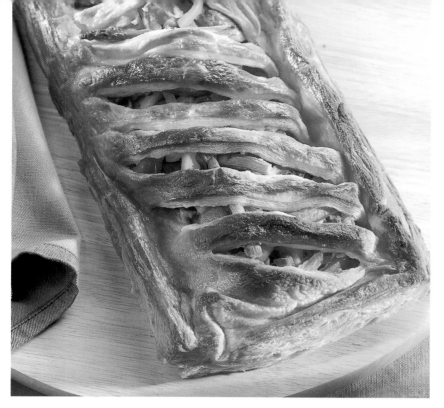

This is a really easy dish to make, but looks impressive. The mixture of vegetables gives the dish a wonderful color and flavor.

Vegetable Jalousie

1 Melt the butter or margarine in a skillet and sauté the leek and garlic, stirring frequently, for 2 minutes. Add the remaining vegetables and cook, stirring, for 3–4 minutes.

2 Add the flour and cook for 1 minute. Remove the pan from the heat and stir in the vegetable bouillon, milk, and white wine. Return the pan to the heat and bring to a boil, stirring, until thickened. Stir in the oregano and season with salt and pepper to taste.

3 Roll out half of the pastry on a lightly floured counter to form a rectangle 15-inches x 6-inches/38-cm x 15-cm.

4 Roll out the other half of the pastry to the same shape, but a little larger all round. Transfer the smaller rectangle to a cookie sheet lined with dampened baking parchment.

5 Spoon the filling evenly on top of the smaller rectangle, leaving a ½-inch/ 1-cm clear margin around the edges.

6 Using a sharp knife, cut parallel diagonal slits across the larger rectangle to within 1-inch/2.5-cm of each of the long edges.

7 Brush the edges of the smaller rectangle with beaten egg and place the larger rectangle on top, pressing the edges firmly together to seal.

8 Brush the whole jalousie with egg to glaze and bake in a preheated oven, 400°F/200°C, for about 30–35 minutes, until well risen and golden.

SERVES 4

1 lb/450 g puff pie dough
flour, for dusting
1 egg, beaten

filling

2 tbsp butter or margarine
1 leek, shredded
2 garlic cloves, crushed
1 red bell pepper, halved, deseeded, and sliced
1 yellow bell pepper, halved, deseeded, and sliced
1 cup sliced mushrooms
3 oz/85 g small asparagus spears
2 tbsp all-purpose flour
6 tbsp Fresh Vegetable Bouillon (see page 16)
6 tbsp milk
4 tbsp dry white wine
1 tbsp chopped fresh oregano
salt and pepper

NUTRITION
Calories *660*; Sugars *7 g*; Protein *11 g*; Carbohydrate *53 g*; Fat *45 g*; Saturates *15 g*

⭐⭐⭐   moderate

🕐   25 mins

🕐   45 mins

This is based on a Moroccan dish in which potatoes are spiced with coriander and cumin and cooked in a lemon sauce.

Potato *and* Lemon Casserole

SERVES 4

scant ½ cup olive oil
2 red onions, cut into 8 wedges
3 garlic cloves, crushed
2 tsp ground cumin
2 tsp ground coriander
pinch of cayenne pepper
1 carrot, sliced thickly
2 small turnips, cut into fourths
1 zucchini, sliced
1 lb/450 g potatoes, sliced thickly
juice and zest of 2 large lemons
1¼ cups Fresh Vegetable Bouillon
   (see page 16)
2 tbsp chopped fresh cilantro
salt and pepper

1 Heat the olive oil in a flameproof casserole. Add the onion and sauté over medium heat, stirring frequently, for 3 minutes.

2 Add the garlic and cook for 30 seconds. Stir in the cumin, ground coriander, and cayenne and cook, stirring constantly, for 1 minute.

3 Add the carrot, turnips, zucchini, and potatoes and stir to coat in the oil.

4 Add the lemon juice and zest and the vegetable bouillon. Season to taste with salt and pepper. Cover and cook over medium heat, stirring occasionally, for 20–30 minutes until tender.

5 Remove the lid, sprinkle in the chopped fresh cilantro and stir well. Serve immediately.

NUTRITION
Calories *338*; Sugars *8 g*; Protein *5 g*;
Carbohydrate *29 g*; Fat *23 g*; Saturates *2 g*

⭐⭐   easy

🍳   15 mins

🕐   35 mins

👨‍🍳 COOK'S TIP

Check the vegetables while they are cooking, because they may begin to stick to the pan. Add a little more boiling water or bouillon if necessary.

A mildly spiced, but richly flavored Indian-style dish full of different textures and flavors. Serve with nan bread to soak up the tasty sauce.

Coconut Vegetable Curry

1 Layer the eggplant in a bowl, sprinkling with salt as you go. Set aside for 30 minutes. Rinse well under running water. Drain and dry. Set aside.

2 Heat the oil in a large pan and gently cook the garlic, chile, gingerroot, onion, and spices for 4–5 minutes.

3 Stir in the tomato paste, bouillon, lemon juice, potatoes, and cauliflower and mix well. Bring to a boil, cover, and simmer for 15 minutes.

4 Stir in the eggplant, okra, peas, and coconut milk and season with salt and pepper to taste. Continue to simmer, uncovered, for a further 10 minutes, until tender. Discard the cardamom pods. Pile the curry onto a warmed serving platter, garnish with flaked coconut, and serve with nan bread.

SERVES 4

1 large eggplant, cut into 1-inch/2.5-cm cubes
2 tbsp vegetable oil
2 garlic cloves, crushed
1 fresh green chile, seeded and chopped finely
1 tsp grated fresh gingerroot
1 onion, chopped finely
2 tsp garam masala
8 cardamom pods
1 tsp ground turmeric
1 tbsp tomato paste
3 cups Fresh Vegetable Bouillon (see page 16)
1 tbsp lemon juice
1½ cups diced potatoes
2 cups small cauliflower flowerets
2 cups okra, trimmed
2 cups frozen peas
⅔ cup coconut milk
salt and pepper
flaked coconut, to garnish
nan bread, to serve

NUTRITION
Calories *159*; Sugars *8 g*; Protein *8 g*;
Carbohydrate *19 g*; Fat *6 g*; Saturates *1 g*

easy

45 mins

35 mins

Quick, simple, nutritious, and a pleasure to eat— what more could you ask of an inexpensive midweek meal?

Bread *and* Butter Savory

SERVES 4

1/4 cup butter
1 bunch scallions, sliced
6 slices of white or whole-wheat bread, crusts removed
1 1/2 cups grated sharp colby cheese
2 eggs
scant 2 cups milk
salt and pepper
flatleaf parsley sprigs, to garnish

1 Lightly grease a 2 3/4 pint/1.5 liter ovenproof dish with a little of the butter.

2 Melt the remaining butter in a small pan. Add the scallions and cook over medium heat, stirring occasionally, until soft and golden.

3 Meanwhile, cut the bread into triangles and place half of them in the base of the dish. Cover with the sliced scallions and top with half the grated colby cheese.

4 Beat together the eggs and milk and season to taste with salt and pepper. Layer the remaining triangles of bread in the dish and carefully pour over the milk mixture. Let soak for 15–20 minutes.

5 Sprinkle the remaining cheese over the soaked bread. Bake in a preheated oven, 375°F/190°C, for 35–40 minutes, until puffed up and golden brown.

6 Garnish with flatleaf parsley and serve immediately.

NUTRITION
Calories *472*; Sugars *7 g*; Protein *22 g*; Carbohydrate *25 g*; Fat *33 g*; Saturates *20 g*

easy

30 mins

45 mins

 COOK'S TIP

You can vary the vegetables used in this savory bake, depending on what you have to hand. Shallots, mushrooms, or tomatoes are all suitable.

These crisp, buttery parcels, filled with nuts and pesto, and served with cranberry sauce, would make a wonderful Sunday lunch.

White Nut Filo Parcels

1 Melt the butter in a skillet, add the onion, and gently cook for 2–3 minutes, until soft, but not brown.

2 Remove from the heat and stir in the nuts, two-thirds of the bread crumbs, the mace, and beaten egg. Season to taste with salt and pepper. Set aside.

3 Place the remaining bread crumbs in a bowl and stir in the egg yolk, pesto sauce, basil, and 1 tablespoon of the melted butter. Mix well.

4 Brush 1 sheet of phyllo with melted butter or margarine. Fold in half and brush again. Repeat with a second sheet and lay it on top of the first one so that it forms a cross.

5 Put one-eighth of the nut mixture in the centre of the pastry. Top with one-eighth of the pesto mixture. Fold over the edges, brushing with more butter, to form a parcel. Brush the top with butter or margarine and transfer to a cookie sheet. Make 8 parcels in the same way and brush with the remaining butter.

6 Bake in a preheated oven, 425°F/220°C, for 15–20 minutes, until golden. Transfer to serving plates, garnish with basil sprigs, and serve with cranberry sauce and steamed vegetables.

SERVES 4

3 tbsp butter
1 large onion, chopped finely
2 cups mixed white nuts, such as pine nuts, unsalted cashew nuts, blanched almonds, and unsalted peanuts, chopped finely
1½ cups fresh white bread crumbs
½ tsp ground mace
1 egg, beaten
1 egg yolk
3 tbsp pesto sauce
2 tbsp chopped fresh basil
9 tbsp butter or margarine, melted
16 sheets phyllo pastry
salt and pepper
fresh basil sprigs, to garnish

to serve
cranberry sauce
steamed vegetables

NUTRITION
Calories 110; Sugars 9 g; Protein 29 g; Carbohydrate 73 g; Fat 80 g; Saturates 15 g

⭐⭐⭐   moderate
🕐   15 mins
🕐   25 mins

This colorful combination of grated root vegetables and mixed bell peppers would make a stunning dinner-party dish.

Root Croustades

SERVES 4

1 orange bell pepper
1 red bell pepper
1 yellow bell pepper
3 tbsp olive oil
2 tbsp red wine vinegar
1 tsp French mustard
1 tsp clear honey
salt and pepper
flatleaf parsley sprigs, to garnish
green vegetables, to serve

croustades

1½ cups potatoes, grated coarsely
1½ cups carrots, grated coarsely
2¼ cups celery root, grated coarsely
1 garlic clove, crushed
1 tbsp lemon juice
2 tbsp butter or margarine, melted
1 egg, beaten
1 tbsp vegetable oil

NUTRITION

Calories *304*; Sugars *17 g*; Protein *6 g*;
Carbohydrate *28 g*; Fat *19 g*; Saturates *3 g*

⭐⭐⭐ moderate

2 hrs 30 mins

1 hr 15 mins

1 Place the bell peppers on a cookie sheet and bake in a preheated oven, 375°F/190°C, for 35 minutes, turning after 20 minutes.

2 Cover with a dish cloth and let cool for 10 minutes.

3 Peel the skin from the cooked bell peppers; cut in half and discard the seeds. Thinly slice the flesh into strips and place in a shallow dish.

4 Put the oil, vinegar, mustard, honey, and seasoning in a small screw-top jar and shake well to mix. Pour over the bell pepper strips, mix well, and let marinate for 2 hours.

5 To make the croustades, put the grated potatoes, carrots, and celery root in a mixing bowl and toss in the crushed garlic and lemon juice.

6 Mix in the melted butter and the egg. Season to taste with salt and pepper. Divide the mixture into 8 and pile on to 2 cookie sheets lined with baking parchment, forming each into a 4-inch/10-cm round. Brush with a little oil.

7 Bake in a preheated oven, 425°F/220°C, for 30–35 minutes, until the croustades are crisp around the edges and golden. Carefully transfer to a warmed serving dish.

8 Heat the bell peppers and the marinade for 2–3 minutes until warmed through. Spoon the bell peppers over the croustades, garnish with flatleaf parsley and serve at once.

A delicious savory roll, stuffed with mozzarella and broccoli. Serve as an entrée or as an appetizer, in which case it would easily serve 6.

Spinach Roulade

1 Wash the spinach and pack, still wet, into a large pan. Add the water. Cover the pan with a tight-fitting lid and cook the spinach over high heat for 4–5 minutes, until reduced and soft. Drain thoroughly, squeezing out excess water. Chop finely and pat dry.

2 Mix the spinach with the egg yolks, seasoning, and nutmeg. Whisk the egg whites until very foamy, but not too stiff, and fold into the spinach mixture.

3 Grease and base-line a 13-inch x 9-inch/32-cm x 23-cm inch jelly roll pan. Spread the spinach mixture in the pan and smooth the surface with a wet spatula. Bake in a preheated oven, 425°F/220°C, for 12–15 minutes, or until firm to the touch and golden brown.

4 Meanwhile, cook the broccoli flowerets in lightly salted boiling water for 4–5 minutes, until just tender. Drain and keep the flowerets warm.

5 Sprinkle Parmesan on a sheet of baking parchment. Turn the base on to it and peel away the top lining paper. Sprinkle with mozzarella and top with broccoli.

6 Hold one end of the paper and roll up the spinach base like a jelly roll. Heat the tomato sauce and spoon on to warmed serving plates. Slice the roulade and place on top of the tomato sauce.

SERVES 4

1 lb/450 g small spinach leaves
2 tbsp water
4 eggs, separated
1/2 tsp ground nutmeg
salt and pepper
1 1/4 cups Tomato Sauce, (see page 16), to serve

filling

1 3/4 cups small broccoli flowerets
1/4 cup freshly grated Parmesan cheese
1 1/2 cups grated mozzarella cheese

NUTRITION

Calories *287*; Sugars *8 g*; Protein *23 g*; Carbohydrate *8 g*; Fat *12 g*; Saturates *6 g*

⭐⭐⭐   moderate

🕐   15 mins

🕐   25 mins

This tastes truly delicious, the flavor of roasted vegetables being entirely different from that of boiled or panfried.

Roasted Bell Pepper Tart

SERVES 4

pie dough
1 generous cup all-purpose flour
pinch of salt
6 tbsp butter or margarine
2 tbsp green pitted olives, chopped finely
3 tbsp cold water

filling
1 red bell pepper
1 green bell pepper
1 yellow bell pepper
2 garlic cloves, crushed
2 tbsp olive oil
1 scant cup grated mozzarella cheese
2 eggs
⅔ cup milk
1 tbsp chopped fresh basil
salt and pepper

1 To make the pastry, sift the flour and salt into a bowl. Rub in the butter, or margarine until the mixture resembles bread crumbs. Add the chopped olives and cold water, bringing the mixture together to form a dough.

2 Roll the dough out on a floured counter and use to line an 8-inch/20-cm loose-based quiche pan. Prick the base with a fork and let chill.

3 Cut the bell peppers in half lengthwise, seed them, and place, skin side uppermost, on a cookie sheet. Mix the garlic and oil and brush over the bell peppers. Cook in a preheated oven, 400°F/200°C, for 20 minutes, or until beginning to char slightly.

4 Let the bell peppers cool slightly and thinly slice. Arrange in the base of the pie shell, layering with the grated mozzarella cheese.

5 Beat the egg and milk and add the basil. Season and pour over the bell peppers. Put the tart on a cookie sheet and return to the oven for 20 minutes, or until set. Serve hot or cold.

NUTRITION
Calories 237; Sugars 3 g; Protein 6 g;
Carbohydrate 20 g; Fat 15 g; Saturates 4 g

✪✪✪   moderate
🕐   25 mins
🕐   40 mins

The red of the tomatoes is a great contrast to the cauliflower and herbs, making this dish appealing to both the eye and the palate.

Cauliflower Bake

1 Cook the cauliflower in a pan of boiling water for 10 minutes. Drain well and reserve. Meanwhile, cook the potatoes in another pan of boiling water for 10 minutes, drain and reserve.

2 To make the sauce, melt the butter in a pan and sauté the leek and garlic for 1 minute. Stir in the flour and cook, stirring constantly, for 1 minute. Remove the pan from the heat and gradually stir in the milk, ½ cup of the grated cheese, the paprika, and flatleaf parsley. Return the pan to the heat and bring to a boil, stirring constantly. Season with salt and pepper.

3 Spoon the cauliflower into a deep casserole. Add the cherry tomatoes and top with the potatoes. Pour the sauce over the potatoes and sprinkle on the remaining cheese.

4 Cook in a preheated oven, 350°F/180°C, for 20 minutes, or until the vegetables are cooked through and the cheese is golden brown and bubbling. Garnish and serve immediately.

SERVES 4

1 lb/450 g cauliflower, broken into florets
1 lb 5 oz/600 g potatoes, cubed
8 cherry tomatoes

sauce

2 tbsp butter or margarine
1 leek, sliced
1 garlic clove, crushed
3 tbsp all-purpose flour
1¼ cups milk
¾ cup grated mixed cheese, such as colby, Parmesan, and Swiss
½ tsp paprika
2 tbsp chopped fresh flatleaf parsley
salt and pepper
chopped fresh parsley, to garnish

NUTRITION

Calories *305*; Sugars *9 g*; Protein *15 g*; Carbohydrate *31 g*; Fat *14 g*; Saturates *6 g*

easy

10 mins

45 mins

🍳 **COOK'S TIP**

This dish could be made with broccoli instead of the cauliflower as an alternative.

This pastry case with a garbanzo bean stuffing is delicious. Served with a sherry sauce, it makes a tasty and impressive entrée.

Garbanzo Bean Roast

SERVES 4

2 cups canned garbanzo beans, drained
1 tsp yeast extract
1½ cups chopped walnuts
2½ cups fresh white bread crumbs
1 onion, chopped finely
1½ cups mushrooms, sliced
¼ cup canned corn kernels, drained
2 garlic cloves, crushed
2 tbsp dry sherry
2 tbsp Fresh Vegetable Bouillon (see page 16)
1 tbsp chopped fresh cilantro
8 oz/225 g prepared puff pie dough
flour, for dusting
1 egg, beaten
2 tbsp milk
salt and pepper

sauce

1 tbsp vegetable oil
1 leek, sliced thinly
4 tbsp dry sherry
⅔ cup Fresh Vegetable Bouillon
   (see page 16)

NUTRITION

Calories *795*; Sugars *9 g*; Protein *24 g*;
Carbohydrate *66 g*; Fat *48 g*; Saturates *3 g*

⭐⭐⭐   moderate

🕒   20 mins

🕐   45 mins

1 Blend the garbanzo beans, yeast extract, nuts, and bread crumbs in a food processor for 30 seconds. In a skillet, sauté the onion and mushrooms in their own juices for 3–4 minutes. Stir in the garbanzo bean mixture, corn kernels, and garlic. Add the sherry, bouillon, cilantro, and seasoning and bind the mixture together. Remove from the heat and let cool.

2 Roll the pie dough out on a floured counter to form a 14-inch x 12-inch/35.5-cm x 30-cm rectangle. Shape the garbanzo bean mixture into a loaf shape and wrap the pie dough around it, sealing the edges. Place seam-side down on a dampened cookie sheet and score the top in a criss-cross pattern. Mix the egg and milk and brush over the pie dough. Cook in a preheated oven, 400°F/200°C, for 25–30 minutes.

3 To make the sauce, heat the oil in a pan and sauté the leek for 5 minutes. Add the sherry and bouillon, bring to a boil, and simmer for 5 minutes. Place the roast on a serving platter, slice and serve with the sauce.

A tasty Mexican-style dish with a melt-in-the-mouth combination of bean curd and avocado, served with a tangy tomato sauce.

Chili Bean Curd

1 Mix the chili powder, paprika, flour, and salt and pepper on a plate and coat the bean curd pieces.

2 Heat the oil in a skillet and gently cook the bean curd for 3–4 minutes, until golden. Remove with a slotted spoon, drain on paper towels, and set aside.

3 Add the onion, garlic, and bell pepper to the oil and cook for 2–3 minutes, until just soft. Drain and set aside.

4 Halve the avocado, remove the pit, and peel. Slice the avocado lengthwise, put in a bowl with the lime juice, and toss to coat.

5 Add the bean curd and onion mixture and gently stir in the chopped tomatoes and half the grated colby cheese. Spoon one-eighth of the filling down the center of each tortilla, top with sour cream, and roll up.

6 Arrange the tortillas, seam-side down, in a shallow ovenproof dish in a single layer.

7 To make the sauce, mix together all the ingredients. Spoon the sauce over the tortillas, sprinkle with the remaining grated cheese, and bake in a preheated oven, 375°F/190°C, for 25 minutes, until the cheese is golden brown and bubbling.

8 Garnish the chili bean curd with cilantro sprigs and serve immediately with pickled jalapeño chiles.

SERVES 4

½ tsp chili powder
1 tsp paprika
2 tbsp all-purpose flour
8 oz/225 g bean curd, cubed
2 tbsp vegetable oil
1 onion, chopped finely
1 garlic clove, crushed
1 large red bell pepper, halved, deseeded, and chopped finely
1 large ripe avocado
1 tbsp lime juice
4 tomatoes, peeled, seeded, and chopped
1 cup grated colby cheese
8 soft flour tortillas
⅔ cup sour cream
salt and pepper
fresh cilantro sprigs to garnish
pickled green jalapeño chiles, to serve

sauce
3½ cups Tomato Sauce (see page 16)
3 tbsp chopped fresh parsley
3 tbsp chopped fresh cilantro

NUTRITION
Calories *806*; Sugars *20 g*; Protein *37 g*;
Carbohydrate *45 g*; Fat *54 g*; Saturates *19 g*

⭐⭐⭐   moderate

🕐   30 mins

🕐   35 mins

Salads

A salad makes a refreshing accompaniment or side dish, but can also make a substantial main course meal. Salads are also a very good source of vitamins and minerals; always use the freshest possible ingredients for maximum flavor, texture, and goodness. Salads are quick to "rustle up" and good for times when you need to prepare a meal in a moment and have to use store-cupboard ingredients. A splash of culinary inspiration and you will find that you have prepared a fantastic salad that you had no idea was lurking in your kitchen! Experiment with new ingredients in order to add taste and interest to ordinary salad leaves. The only limit is your imagination!

This is a colorful salad with a Mexican theme, using beans, tomatoes, and avocado. The chili dressing adds a little kick.

Bean *and* Tomato Salad

SERVES 4

1 lollo rosso lettuce
2 ripe avocados
2 tsp lemon juice
4 medium tomatoes
1 onion
¾ cup mixed canned beans, drained

dressing

4 tbsp olive oil
dash of chili oil
2 tbsp garlic wine vinegar
pinch of superfine sugar
pinch of chili powder
1 tbsp chopped fresh parsley

1 Line a large serving bowl with the lettuce leaves.

2 Using a sharp knife, cut the avocados in half and remove the pits. Thinly slice the flesh and immediately sprinkle with the lemon juice.

3 Thinly slice the tomatoes and onion and push the onion out into rings. Arrange the avocado, tomatoes, and onion around the salad bowl, leaving a space in the center.

4 Spoon the beans into the center of the salad and whisk the dressing ingredients together. Pour the dressing over the salad and serve.

NUTRITION

Calories *307*; Sugars *7 g*; Protein *5 g*; Carbohydrate *13 g*; Fat *26 g*; Saturates *5 g*

⭐ very easy

🕐 10–15 mins

🕐 0 mins

👨‍🍳 COOK'S TIP

The lemon juice is sprinkled on to the avocados to prevent discoloration when in contact with the air. For this reason, the salad should be prepared, assembled, and served quite quickly.

Couscous is a type of semolina made from durum wheat. It is wonderful in salads, as it readily takes up the flavor of the dressing.

Moroccan Salad

1 Put the couscous into a bowl and pour over boiling water to cover. Let it soak for about 15 minutes to swell the grains, then stir gently with a fork to separate them.

2 Add the scallions, green bell pepper, cucumber, garbanzo beans, and golden raisins to the couscous, stirring to combine. Season with salt and pepper.

3 To make the dressing, place the orange zest, mint, and yogurt in a bowl and mix together until well combined. Pour over the couscous mixture and stir to mix well.

4 Using a sharp serrated knife, remove the peel and pith from the oranges. Cut the flesh into segments, removing all the membrane.

5 Arrange the lettuce leaves on 4 serving plates. Divide the couscous mixture between the plates and arrange the orange segments on top. Garnish with sprigs of fresh mint and serve.

SERVES 4

1 cup couscous
1 bunch scallions, chopped finely
1 small green bell pepper, seeded and chopped
4-inch/10-cm piece of cucumber, chopped
1 cup canned garbanzo beans, rinsed and drained
½ cup golden raisins or raisins
2 oranges
salt and pepper
fresh mint sprigs, to garnish
lettuce leaves, to serve

dressing
finely grated zest of 1 orange
1 tbsp chopped fresh mint
⅔ cup plain yogurt

NUTRITION
Calories 195; Sugars 15 g; Protein 8 g;
Carbohydrate 40 g; Fat 2 g; Saturates 0.3 g

✪✪✪   moderate
🕐   30 mins
🕐   0 mins

This attractive-looking salad can be served with a couple of vegetable kebabs for a delicious light lunch or an informal supper.

Middle Eastern Salad

SERVES 4

1¹/₂ cup canned garbanzo beans
1 medium cucumber
4 carrots, sliced thinly
1 bunch scallions, chopped into small pieces
¹/₂ tsp salt
¹/₂ tsp pepper
3 tbsp lemon juice
1 red bell pepper, halved, deseeded, and sliced

1 Drain the garbanzo beans and place them in a large salad bowl.

2 Thickly slice the cucumber and then cut the slices into quarters. Add the carrots, scallions, and cucumber to the garbanzo beans and mix.

3 Season to taste with the salt and pepper and sprinkle with the lemon juice. Toss the salad ingredients together gently, using 2 serving spoons.

4 Arrange the slices of red bell pepper decoratively on top of the garbanzo bean salad. Serve the salad immediately or chill in the refrigerator and serve when required.

NUTRITION
Calories 163; Sugars 12 g; Protein 8 g;
Carbohydrate 27 g; Fat 3 g; Saturates 0.4 g

⭐ very easy

🕐 15 mins

🕐 0 mins

🍳 COOK'S TIP

This salad would also be delicious made with *ful medames*. If they are not available canned, use 1 cup dried, soaked for 5 hours and simmered for 2¹/₂ hours.

Pecan nuts with their slightly bitter flavor are mixed with sweet potatoes to make a sweet and sour salad with an interesting texture.

Sweet Potato *and* Nut Salad

1 Cook the sweet potatoes in a large pan of boiling water for 10–15 minutes, until tender. Drain thoroughly and let cool.

2 When the potatoes have cooled, stir in the sliced celery, celery root, scallions, and pecan nuts.

3 Line a salad plate with the endive leaves and sprinkle with lemon juice.

4 Spoon the sweet potato mixture into the center of the leaves.

5 In a small bowl, whisk together the vegetable oil, garlic wine vinegar, sugar, and chopped thyme, then pour the dressing over the salad.

6 Serve the sweet potato and nut salad immediately, garnished with fresh thyme sprigs.

SERVES 4

2³⁄₄ cups diced sweet potatoes
2 celery stalks, sliced
1 firmly packed cup celery root, grated
2 scallions, sliced
¹⁄₂ cup pecan nuts, chopped
2 heads Belgian endive, separated
1 tsp lemon juice
fresh thyme sprigs, to garnish

dressing
4 tbsp vegetable oil
1 tbsp garlic wine vinegar
1 tsp soft light brown sugar
2 tsp chopped fresh thyme

NUTRITION
Calories *330*; Sugars *5 g*; Protein *4 g*;
Carbohydrate *36 g*; Fat *20 g*; Saturates *2 g*

⭐⭐⭐   moderate
🕐   15 mins
🕐   10-15 mins

🧑‍🍳 **COOK'S TIP**

Sweet potatoes do not store as well as ordinary potatoes. Store them in a cool, dark place (not the refrigerator) and use within 1 week of purchase.

This is a well-known and very popular Indonesian salad of mixed vegetables with a peanut dressing.

Gado Gado

SERVES 4

1 1/2 cups shredded white cabbage
1 cup green beans, cut into 3
1 cup carrots, cut into matchsticks
scant cup cauliflower flowerets
1 cup beansprouts

dressing
1/3 cup vegetable oil
1/2 cup unsalted peanuts
2 garlic cloves, crushed
1 small onion, chopped finely
1/2 tsp chili powder
1/2 tsp light brown sugar
1 3/4 cups water
juice of 1/2 lemon
salt
sliced scallions, to garnish

1 Cook the vegetables separately in a pan of salted boiling water for 4–5 minutes each, drain well, and chill.

2 To make the dressing, heat the oil in a skillet and cook the peanuts, tossing frequently, for 3–4 minutes.

3 Remove the peanuts from the skillet with a slotted spoon and drain on paper towels. Process in a food processor or crush with a rolling pin until a fine mixture is formed.

4 Leave 1 tablespoon of oil in the skillet and cook the garlic and onion for 1 minute. Add the chili powder, sugar, a pinch of salt, and the water and bring to a boil.

5 Stir the peanuts into the sauce. Reduce the heat and simmer for 4–5 minutes, until the sauce thickens. Add the lemon juice and let cool.

6 Arrange the vegetables in a serving dish and spoon the peanut dressing into the center. Garnish with the sliced scallions and serve.

NUTRITION
Calories *392*; Sugars *8 g*; Protein *9 g*;
Carbohydrate *11 g*; Fat *35 g*; Saturates *5 g*

easy

10 mins

25 mins

Fresh thin green beans are combined with soybeans and red kidney beans in a chive and tomato dressing to make a tasty salad.

Three-Bean Salad

1 Put the olive oil, lemon juice, tomato paste, light malt vinegar, and chopped fresh chives into a large bowl and mix thoroughly. Set aside until required.

2 Cook the thin green beans in a small pan of lightly salted boiling water for 4–5 minutes. Drain, refresh under cold water to prevent any further cooking, and drain well again. Pat dry with absorbent paper towels.

3 Add all the beans to the dressing, stirring well to mix.

4 Add the tomatoes, scallions, and feta cheese to the bean mixture, tossing gently to coat in the dressing. Season to taste with salt and pepper.

5 Arrange the salad greens on serving plates. Pile the bean salad on top, garnish with extra chives, and serve.

SERVES 6

3 tbsp olive oil
1 tbsp lemon juice
1 tbsp tomato paste
1 tbsp light malt vinegar
1 tbsp chopped fresh chives,
   plus extra to garnish
1½ cups thin green beans, cut into thirds
1½ cups canned soybeans, rinsed
   and drained
1½ cups canned red kidney beans, rinsed
   and drained
2 tomatoes, chopped
4 scallions, trimmed and chopped
1 cup feta cheese, cut into cubes
salt and pepper
mixed salad greens, to serve

NUTRITION
Calories *276*; Sugars *7 g*; Protein *18 g*;
Carbohydrate *18 g*; Fat *15 g*; Saturates *4 g*

⊛⊛   easy
☺   10 mins
🕐   5 mins

👨‍🍳 COOK'S TIP

For a more substantial light meal, top the salad with 2–3 sliced hard-cooked eggs and serve with crusty bread to soak up the juices.

This delicious salad combines soft goat cheese with walnut halves, served on a bed of mixed salad leaves.

Warm Goat Cheese Salad

SERVES 4

¾ cup walnut halves
mixed salad leaves
1 cup soft goat cheese
snipped fresh chives, to garnish

dressing

6 tbsp walnut oil
3 tbsp white wine vinegar
1 tbsp clear honey
1 tsp Dijon mustard
pinch of ground ginger
salt and pepper

1 To make the dressing, whisk together the walnut oil, wine vinegar, honey, mustard, and ginger in a small pan. Season to taste with salt and pepper.

2 Heat the dressing gently, stirring occasionally, until warm. Add the walnut halves and continue to heat for 3–4 minutes.

3 Arrange the salad leaves on 4 serving plates and place spoonfuls of goat cheese on top. Lift the walnut halves from the dressing with a draining spoon and scatter them over the salad leaves.

4 Transfer the warm dressing to a small pitcher. Sprinkle chives over the salads and serve with the dressing.

NUTRITION
Calories *408*; Sugars *8 g*; Protein *9 g*; Carbohydrate *8 g*; Fat *38 g*; Saturates *8 g*

very easy

5 mins

5 mins

🧑‍🍳 **COOK'S TIP**

You could also use a ewe's milk cheese, such as feta, in this recipe for a slightly sharper flavor.

Small new potatoes, served warm in a delicious dressing. The nutritional information is for the potato salad with the curry dressing only.

Three-Way Potato Salad

1 To make the Light Curry Dressing, heat the vegetable oil in a pan. Add the curry paste and onion and cook, stirring frequently, until the onion is soft. Remove from the heat and let cool slightly.

2 Mix together the mango chutney, yogurt, cream, and mayonnaise. Add the curry mixture and blend together. Season with salt and pepper.

3 To make the Vinaigrette Dressing, whisk the oil, vinegar, mustard, sugar, and basil together in a small pitcher or bowl. Season with salt and pepper.

4 To make the Parsley Cream, combine the mayonnaise, sour cream, scallions, and parsley, mixing well. Season with salt and pepper.

5 Cook the potatoes in lightly salted boiling water until just tender. Drain well and let cool for 5 minutes, then add the chosen dressing, tossing to coat.

6 Serve the salads garnished with fresh herbs, spooning a little light cream on to the potatoes if you have used the curry dressing.

SERVES 4

1 lb/450 g new potatoes (for each dressing)
fresh herbs, to garnish

light curry dressing
1 tbsp vegetable oil
1 tbsp medium curry paste
1 small onion, chopped
1 tbsp mango chutney, chopped
6 tbsp plain yogurt
3 tbsp light cream
2 tbsp mayonnaise
salt and pepper
1 tbsp light cream, to garnish

vinaigrette dressing
6 tbsp hazelnut oil
3 tbsp cider vinegar
1 tsp whole-grain mustard
1 tsp superfine sugar
few fresh basil leaves, torn

parsley cream
3 tbsp light mayonnaise
$\frac{2}{3}$ cup sour cream
4 scallions, chopped finely
1 tbsp chopped fresh parsley

NUTRITION
Calories *310*; Sugars *12 g*; Protein *6 g*;
Carbohydrate *31 g*; Fat *19 g*; Saturates *4 g*

✪✪✪   moderate
🕐   15 mins
🕐   20 mins

Use any mixture of beans you have to hand in this recipe, but the wider the variety, the more colorful the salad.

Mixed Bean *and* Apple Salad

SERVES 4

8 oz/225 g new potatoes, scrubbed and cut into fourths

1½ cups mixed canned beans, such as red kidney beans, small cannellini beans, and borlotti beans, drained and rinsed

1 red eating apple, diced and tossed in 1 tbsp lemon juice

1 yellow bell pepper, halved, deseeded, and diced

1 shallot, sliced

½ fennel bulb, sliced

oakleaf lettuce leaves

dressing

1 tbsp red wine vinegar

2 tbsp olive oil

1½ tsp mild yellow mustard

1 garlic clove, crushed

2 tsp chopped fresh thyme

1 Cook the potatoes in a pan of boiling water for 15 minutes until tender. Drain and transfer to a large bowl.

2 Add the mixed beans to the potatoes, with the diced apple, yellow bell pepper, shallot, and fennel. Mix thoroughly, taking care not to break up the cooked potatoes.

3 To make the dressing, whisk all the dressing ingredients together, until thoroughly combined, then pour it over the potato salad.

4 Line a serving plate or salad bowl with the oakleaf lettuce leaves and spoon the potato mixture into the center. Serve the salad immediately.

NUTRITION

Calories *183*; Sugars *8 g*; Protein *6 g*; Carbohydrate *26 g*; Fat *7 g*; Saturates *1 g*

⭐ very easy

🍳 20 mins

🕐 15 mins

👨‍🍳 **COOK'S TIP**

You could use Dijon or whole-grain mustard in place of mild yellow mustard for a different flavor.

Lightly steamed vegetables taste superb served slightly warm in a marinade of olive oil, white wine, vinegar, and fresh herbs.

Marinated Vegetable Salad

1 Put the carrots, celery, sugar snap peas, fennel, and asparagus into a steamer and cook over gently simmering water for 3–5 minutes, until just tender. It is important that they retain a little bite.

2 Meanwhile, make the dressing. Combine the olive oil, wine, vinegar, and chopped fresh herbs, whisking until thoroughly mixed. Season to taste with salt and pepper.

3 When the vegetables are cooked, transfer them to a serving dish and immediately pour the dressing over them. The hot vegetables will absorb the flavor of the dressing as they cool.

4 Spread out the sunflower seeds on a cookie sheet and toast them under a preheated broiler for 3–4 minutes or until lightly browned and are beginning to smell fragrant. Sprinkle the toasted sunflower seeds over the vegetables.

5 Serve the salad while the vegetables are still slightly warm, garnished with fresh dill sprigs.

SERVES 6

18 baby carrots
2 celery hearts, cut into 4 pieces
1 ½ cups sugar snap peas
1 fennel bulb, sliced
6 oz/175 g small asparagus spears
4½ tsp sunflower seeds
fresh dill sprigs, to garnish

dressing
¼ cup extra virgin olive oil
¼ cup dry white wine
2 tbsp white wine vinegar
1 tbsp chopped fresh dill
1 tbsp chopped fresh parsley
salt and pepper

NUTRITION
Calories 114; Sugars 4 g; Protein 3 g;
Carbohydrate 5 g; Fat 9 g; Saturates 1 g

easy

10 mins

10 mins

This refreshing salad must be assembled just before serving to prevent all of the ingredients being colored pink by the beet.

Alfalfa *and* Beetroot Salad

SERVES 4

2 cups tightly packed young spinach leaves
3 oz/85 g alfalfa sprouts
2 celery stalks, sliced
4 cooked beets, cut into 8 wedges

dressing
4 tbsp olive oil
4½ tsp garlic wine vinegar
1 garlic clove, crushed
2 tsp honey
1 tbsp chopped fresh chives

1 If the spinach leaves are large, tear them into smaller pieces. (Cutting them would bruise them.) Place the spinach and alfalfa sprouts in a large bowl and mix together.

2 Add the celery and mix well. Toss in the beets and mix again.

3 To make the dressing, mix the oil, wine vinegar, garlic, honey, and chopped chives in a small bowl.

4 Pour the dressing over the salad, toss well, and serve immediately.

NUTRITION
Calories *139*; Sugars *7 g*; Protein *2 g*;
Carbohydrate *8 g*; Fat *11 g*; Saturates *2 g*

very easy

10 mins

0 mins

🍳 COOK'S TIP

Add the segments of 1 large orange to the salad to make it even more colorful and refreshing. Replace the garlic wine vinegar with plain white wine vinegar and use a different flavored oil such as chili or herb, if you prefer.

This salad uses lots of green-colored ingredients which look and taste wonderful with the minty yogurt dressing.

Mint *and* Zucchini Salad

1 Cook the zucchini batons and beans in a pan of lightly salted boiling water for 7–8 minutes. Drain, rinse under cold running water, and drain again. Set aside to cool completely.

2 Mix the zucchini and beans with the green bell pepper strips, celery, and arugula in a large serving bowl.

3 To make the dressing, combine the yogurt, garlic, and chopped fresh mint in a small bowl. Season with pepper to taste.

4 Spoon the dressing onto the salad and serve immediately.

SERVES 4

2 zucchini, cut into batons
1¼ cups green beans, cut into thirds
1 green bell pepper, halved, deseeded, and cut into strips
2 celery stalks, sliced
1 bunch of arugula

dressing
scant 1 cup plain yogurt
1 garlic clove, crushed
2 tbsp chopped fresh mint
pepper

NUTRITION
Calories *49*; Sugars *5 g*; Protein *4 g*; Carbohydrate *6 g*; Fat *1 g*; Saturates *0 g*

⭐ very easy
🍽 30 mins
🕐 7–8 mins

🍳 **COOK'S TIP**

The salad must be served as soon as the yogurt dressing has been added—the dressing will start to separate if it is kept for any length of time.

This refreshing fruit-based salad is perfect for a hot summer's day and would be perfect served with roast vegetables.

Melon *and* Strawberry Salad

SERVES 4

½ iceberg lettuce, shredded
1 small honeydew melon
2 cups strawberries, sliced
2-inch/5-cm piece of cucumber, sliced thinly
fresh mint sprigs to garnish

dressing

scant 1 cup plain yogurt
2-inch/5-cm piece of cucumber, peeled
a few fresh mint leaves
½ tsp finely grated lime or lemon peel
pinch of superfine sugar
3–4 ice cubes

1 Arrange the shredded lettuce on 4 serving plates.

2 Cut the melon lengthwise into quarters. Scoop out the seeds and cut through the flesh down to the skin at 1-inch/2.5-cm intervals. Cut the melon close to the skin and detach the flesh.

3 Place the chunks of melon on the beds of lettuce with the strawberries and cucumber slices.

4 To make the dressing, put the yogurt, cucumber, mint leaves, lime peel, superfine sugar, and ice cubes into a blender or food processor. Blend together for about 15 seconds until smooth. Alternatively, chop the cucumber and mint finely, crush the ice cubes, and combine these with the other ingredients.

5 Serve the salad with a little dressing poured over it. Garnish with fresh mint sprigs.

NUTRITION
Calories *112*; Sugars *22 g*; Protein *5 g*;
Carbohydrate *22 g*; Fat *1 g*; Saturates *0.3 g*

⭐ very easy

🕑 15 mins

🕐 0 mins

👨‍🍳 **COOK'S TIP**

Omit the ice cubes from the dressing if you prefer, but make sure that the ingredients are well-chilled. This will ensure that the finished dressing is really cool.

A little freshly grated gingerroot mixed with creamy yogurt and honey makes a perfect dressing for this refreshing salad.

Melon *and* Mango Salad

1 To make the dressing, for the melon, whisk together the yogurt, honey, and gingerroot in a small bowl.

2 Halve the melon, scoop out the seeds with a spoon, and discard. Slice, peel, and dice the flesh. Place in a bowl with the grapes.

3 Slice the mango on each side of its large flat pit. On each mango half, slash the flesh into a criss-cross pattern down to, but not through the skin. Push the skin from underneath to turn the mango halves inside out. Now remove the flesh and add to the melon mixture.

4 Arrange the arugula and lettuce leaves on 4 serving plates.

5 Make the dressing for the salad leaves by whisking together the olive oil and vinegar with a little salt and pepper. Drizzle over the salad greens.

6 Divide the melon mixture among the 4 plates and spoon the yogurt dressing over it.

7 Scoop the seeds out of the passion fruit and sprinkle them over the salads. Serve immediately or chill in the refrigerator until required.

SERVES 4

1 cantaloupe melon
12 black grapes, halved and seeded
12 green grapes
1 large mango
1 bunch of arugula, trimmed
iceberg lettuce leaves, shredded
2 tbsp olive oil
1 tbsp apple vinegar
1 passion fruit
salt and pepper

dressing
⅔ cup lowfat plain yogurt
1 tbsp honey
1 tsp grated fresh gingerroot

NUTRITION
Calories *189*; Sugars *30 g*; Protein *5 g*;
Carbohydrate *30 g*; Fat *7 g*; Saturates *1 g*

⭐⭐   easy

🕐   15 mins

🕐   20 mins

Index

A

alfalfa and beetroot salad 170
almond and sesame roasts 133
aloo chat 108
amino acids 7–9
appetizers 40–59
apple and cider vinegar dressing 17
aruglia 13
asparagus 12
    soup 32
avocados 14
    and vegetable soup 33

B

bakes
    bread and butter savoury 150
    brown rice gratin 82
    cauliflower 155
    cheese and potato layer 144
    creamy fennel 145
    potato and eggplant gratin 146
    potato-topped lentil 135
    root croustades 152
    tomato and pasta 88
    vegetable jalousie 147
    white nut filo parcels 151
basic recipes 16–17
bean curd
    chili 157
    tempura 53
    vegetable strudel 138
bean soup 37
béchamel sauce 16
Belgian endives 13
bell peppers 11, 14
    and chili soup 24
    tart 154
bhajis 54
Bombay bowl 81
bread and butter savoury 150
broccoli 12
    and potato soup 30
brown rice gratin 82
Brussels sprouts 12
bubble and squeak 122
buck rarebit 78
bulgar pilau 102
burgers and chips 66
buttered nut and lentil dip 43

C

cabbage 12

cakes
    pan potato 120
    vegetable 142
calcium 7, 9
cannelloni, vegetable 89
carbohydrates 7
carrots 7, 12
cashew nut paella 124
casseroles
    lentil and rice 130
    potato and lemon 148
    vegetable hotpot 136
    winter vegetable cobbler 131
cauliflower 12
    bake 155
celery root 13
cheese 9
    feta patties 127
    feta tartlets 48
    fondue 84
    garlic and herb pâté 44
    and onion rostis 83
    and potato layer bake 144
    warm goat cheese salad 166
chili bean curd 157
Chinese cabbage 12
cholesterol 9
chow mein 95
coconut vegetable curry 149
corn patties 77
couscous, vegetable 101
cream cheese and herb soup 39
creamy baked fennel 145
crêpes, vegetable 64
cress and cheese tartlets 76
croquettes, lentil 79
cucumbers 13
    dressing 17
curried dishes
    coconut vegetable 149
    green curry with tempeh 118
    lentil soup 36
    parsnip soup 27
    potato and vegetable 115
    tomato 117
    vegetables 114

D

dairy products 9
deep South rice and beans 98
dips
    buttered nut and lentil dip 43
    heavenly garlic 42

dressings
    apple & cider vinegar 17
    cucumber 17
    green herb 17
    sesame 17
    tomato 17
    warm walnut 17

E

eggplants 14
enchiladas, vegetable 63
escarole 13

F

falafel 67
fats 7
fava beans 12
fennel 12
    creamy baked 145
    marinated 73
feta cheese
    patties 127
    tartlets 48
fibre 7
fiery salsa 51
fondue, three-cheese 84
fried rice with spicy beans 119
fritters, potato 69

G

gado gado 164
garbanzo beans
    aloo chat 108
    falafel 67
    hummus toasts 49
    roast 156
garlic 7
    dip 42
    mushroom pakoras 56
    mushrooms on toast 74
gazpacho 22
globe artichokes 12
    stuffed 72
goat cheese salad 166
gratin
    brown rice 82
    potato and eggplant 146
green curry with tempeh 118
green herb dressing 17
green vegetables 12
    gougère 137

H

healthy eating 7–9
heavenly garlic dip 42
hotpot, vegetable 136
hummus toasts with olives 49
Hyderabad pickles 55

I

Indian dishes
    bean soup 38
    omelet 75
    potato and pea soup 31
iron 7, 9
Italian vegetable tart 140

J

jambalaya, vegetable 65
Jerusalem artichokes 13

K

kabobs, kofta 111
kale 12
kidney bean kiev 121
kitchouri 106
kofta kabobs 111

L

lasagna, vegetable 90
leafy vegetables 12
leeks 13
    and herb soufflé 143
    potato and carrot soup 29
legumes 9, 19, 87, 108–11
lentils
    buttered nut dip 43
    croquettes 79
    pâté 45
    potato-topped bake 135
    and rice casserole 130
    roast 132
    soup 36
    tarka dhal 109
lettuce 13
light meals 60–85
lysine 9

M

magnesium 7
marinated dishes
    fennel 73

vegetable salad 169
melons
    and mango salad 173
    and strawberry salad 172
Mexican dishes
    chili corn pie 135
    salad 160
Middle Eastern salad 162
minerals 7, 9
mini vegetable puff pastries 58
mint and zucchini salad 171
mixed beans
    and apple salad 168
    pan-fry 70
    pâté 46
mixed bhajis 54
mixed mushroom patties 80
mooli 13
Moroccan salad 161
muffins, vegetable-topped 62
mushrooms
    garlic 74
    and garlic soufflés 59
    pakoras 56
    and spinach puffs 139
    stuffed 71
    tarts 141
muttar paneer 116

N

noodles 9
    chow mein 95
    stir-fried Japanese 93
    Thai-style stir-fried 92
nut and lentil dip 43

O

omelet, Indian-style 75
onions 7, 13
    à la Grecque 50
    soup 26

P

pakora, garlicky mushroom 56
pan potato cake 120
paprika chips 69
parsnips 13
    soup 27
pasta 7, 9, 88–91
    vegetable pasta stir-fry 125
pâtés
    cheese, garlic and herb 44

lentil 45
mixed bean 46
patties
    corn 77
    feta cheese 127
    mixed mushroom 80
peas 12
pickles, Hyderabad 55
pie, Mexican chili corn 135
pilau rice 103
plum tomato soup 21
pole beans 12
polyunsaturated fats 7
potassium 7
potatoes 13
    cake 120
    and eggplant gratin 146
    fritters with relish 69
    and lemon casserole 148
    paprika crisps 69
    and pea soup 31
    potato-topped lentil bake 135
    three-way salad 167
    and vegetable curry 115
protein 7, 9
pumpkins 14
    soup 23

R

radicchio 13
radishes 14
rice 7, 9
    cashew nut paella 124
    deep South rice and beans 98
    fried rice with spicy beans 119
    gratin 82
    kitchouri 106
    pilau 103
    risotto in shells 97
    risotto verde 96
    special fried 94
    spiced basmati pilau 99
    spinach and nut pilau 105
    Thai jasmine 100
    tomato 104
    vegetable biryani 107
risotto
    in shells 97
    verde 96
roast bell pepper tart 154
roasts
    almond and sesame 133
    garbanzo 156

lentil 132
rocket 14
root vegetables 12–13
    croustades 152
rostis, cheese and onion 83
roulade, spinach 153
rutabagas 13

S

salads
    alfalfa and beetroot 170
    gado gado 164
    marinated vegetable 169
    melon and strawberry 172
    Mexican 160
    Middle Eastern 162
    mint and zucchini 171
    Mixed bean and apple 168
    Moroccan 161
    sweet potato and nut 163
    three-bean 165
    three-way potato 167
    vegetables 13–14
    warm goat cheese 166
salsa, fiery 51
samosas 57
saturated fats 7
sauces
    béchamel 16
    tomato 16
sauté, summer vegetables 123
scallions 13
sesame dressing 17
shallots 13
snow peas 12
soufflés
    leek and herb 143
    mushroom and garlic 59
soups
    asparagus 32
    avocado and vegetable 33
    bean 37
    bell pepper and chili 24
    broccoli and potato 30
    cream cheese and herb 39
    curried lentil soup 36
    curried parsnip 27
    gazpacho 22
    Indian bean 38
    Indian potato and pea 31
    leek, potato, and carrot 29
    plum tomato 21
    pumpkin 23

spinach and mascarpone 28
stilton and walnut 25
thick onion 26
vegetable and corn chowder 35
Vichyssoise 34
winter 20
special fried rice 94
spiced basmati pilau 99
spinach 12
    filo baskets 47
    and mascarpone soup 28
    and nut pasta 91
    and nut pilau 105
    roulade 153
spring rolls 52
squashes 14
stilton and walnut soup 25
stir-fries
    green curry with tempeh 118
    Japanese noodles 93
    Thai-style noodles 92
    vegetable pasta 125
stock 16
strudel, vegetable and bean curd 138
stuffed dishes
    globe artichokes 72
    mushrooms 71
sugar snap peas 12
summer squashes 14
summer vegetable sauté 123
sweet potatoes 13
    and nut salad 163
sweet and sour vegetables 126

T

tahini cream 16
tarka dhal 109
tarts
    cress and cheese 76
    feta cheese 48
    Italian vegetable 140
    mushroom 141
    roast bell pepper 154
Thai dishes
    jasmine rice 100
    stir-fried noodles 92
thick onion soup 26
three-bean salad 165
three-cheese fondue 84
three-way potato salad 167
tomatoes 11, 14
    curry 117
    dressing 17

and pasta bake 88
rice 104
sauce 16
soup 21
toovat dhal 110

V

vegans 9
vegetables 7, 9
    and bean curd strudels 138
    biryani 107
    burgers and chips 66
    buying/preparing 10
    cake 142
    cannelloni 89
    coconut curry 149
    and corn chowder 35
    couscous 101
    crêpes 64
    curry 114
    enchiladas 63
    fresh stock 16
    green gougère 137
    hotpot 136
    Italian tart 140
    jalousie 147
    jambalaya 65
    lasagna 90
    marinated salad 169
    muffins 62
    pasta stir-fry 125
    puff pastries 58
    summer sauté 123
    sweet and sour 126
    types 12–14
    winter cobbler 131
Vichyssoise 34
vitamins 7, 9

W

walnut dressing 17
warm goat cheese salad 166
watercress 14
white nut filo parcels 151
winter dishes
    soup 20
    vegetable cobbler 131

Z

zucchini 14
    and mint salad 171